FIELD GUIDE

for

home inspectors

◆

A quick reference for finding the age of 154 brands of HVAC systems, water heaters, and electrical panels, plus 210 code standards for site-built and manufactured homes, and life expectancy ratings of 195 home components

◆

Greg Madsen and Richard M. McGarry

Other Books by Richard M. McGarry and Greg Madsen

Handbook for Manufactured Home Inspectors
Good Buy or Big Mistake?
Scale Elements for Design Elevations
Tracing File for Interior and Architectural Rendering
Gay Key West - A History
Faces of Old Key West 1918
Marker Magic

Field Guide for Home Inspectors
Copyright © 2023 by McGarry and Madsen
All photos are by authors, licensed, or in public domain.

Published by McGarry and Madsen
16822 SE 92nd Danna Ave, The Villages, FL 32162
mcgarryandmadsen@mac.com

Distributed to the trade by Ingram Content Group
ISBN: 978-0-9886651-8-7
Library of Congress Control Number: 2023918489

Table of Contents

Introduction

This book is a result of the research and note-taking from a couple of decades of home inspections. It's a resource we wish we had years ago, and will be using ourselves regularly. The entries are short and to the point for quick reference on the job.

The book is not a complete, exhaustive volume—which would require hundreds of pages just for code standards—and it only covers things that are likely to be visible in a home inspection. We hope you find it useful.

— Greg Madsen and Richard M. McGarry

hvac

Affinity - 2nd and 4th digits of serial number are year of manufacture.

ZYZH03611CA

Serial No. **W1D1945273**

R410A

• •

Airdach - Look for the scan-bar/QR-code strip below the data sticker on the unit. The year of manufacture is the third and fourth numbers in the sequence at the lower right.

SMM0WDN3LWW081000351
8G0-20097203

20220305

• •

Aire-Flo - 3rd and 4th numbers in serial number are year of manufacture.

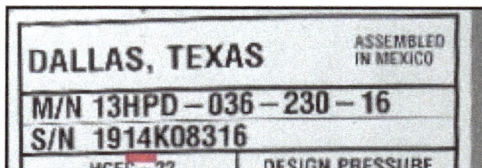

DALLAS, TEXAS   ASSEMBLED IN MEXICO

M/N 13HPD – 036 – 230 – 16
S/N 1914K08316

DESIGN PRESSURE

• •

Airquest - first two numbers after a single letter are year of manufacture. If does not begin with a single letter, then 3rd and 4th numbers. Discontinued after 1999.

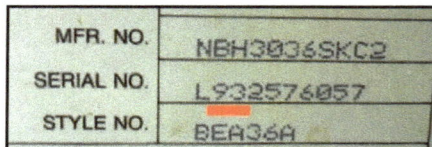

MFR. NO.   NBH3036SKC2
SERIAL NO.   L932576057
STYLE NO.   BEA36A

• •

Airtemp central HVAC systems were manufactured by Chrysler, and then Fedders, both in the 1970s and the units are now long gone. The brand is currently made by Nortek (formerly Nordyne), and the 4th and 5th digits of serial number are year of manufacture. See Nordyne for example.

• •

Allied Air - two versions. The first one uses the third and fourth number for the year of manufacture, like at right. The second system puts the year in the 7th and 8th

MOD. NO. **PRHP1460P – 2A**
SER. NO. **1618B13260**
ABOVE MODEL & SERIAL NO. REQUIRED T

number (3rd and 4th from the end) of the serial number, so 5123610221 was produced in 2002.

Amana - First two numbers of serial number are year of manufacture. Manufactured by Goodman.

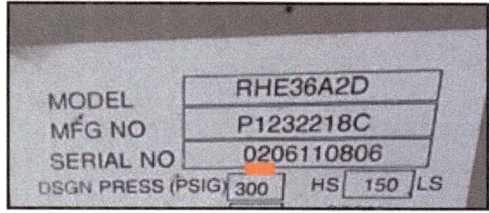

MODEL	RHE36A2D
MFG NO	P1232218C
SERIAL NO	0206110806
DSGN PRESS (PSIG) 300	HS 150 LS

• •

American Standard - Most units state date of manufacture in upper right of data plate. But, if the date is illegible, it is also encoded in the serial number. Either the first number or the first two numbers are the year of manufacture and here's two examples.

The only exception to this simple system is that some models manufactured during the 1980's thru the 90's, and specifically the Allegiance and Heritage lines, use the first letter of the serial number to encode the year of manufacture.

W = 1983, X = 1984, Y = 1985, Z = 1986, B = 1987,
C = 1988, D = 1989, E = 1990, F = 1991, G = 1992,
H = 1993, J = 1994, K = 1995, L = 1996, M = 1997,
N = 1998, P = 1999, R = 2000

So the "K" in the serial number of the data plate shown below indicates that the condenser was made in 1995. But, of course, it is also stated outright in the upper right of the label.

• •

Ameristar - First two numbers of serial number are year of manufacture.

AquaTherm - See First Co.

• •

Arcoaire - First two numbers after an initial letter of serial number are year of manufacture.

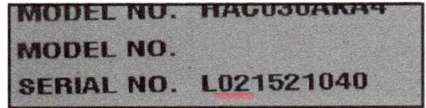

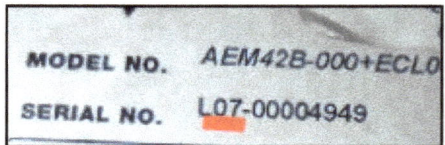

MODEL NO.   HAC030AKA4
MODEL NO.
SERIAL NO.   L021521040

• •

Armstrong, Armstrong Air or Magic Chef - The 8th digit of the serial number (next to last), which will be a letter, using the following code for year of manufacture: A=1980, B=1981, C=1982, D=1983, E=1984,

SERIAL NUMBER
A 10322EDB
CODE   STAMPING NO.
331328063

F=1985, G=1986, H=1987, J=1988, K=1989, L=1990, M=1991, N=1992. So "D" means 1983.

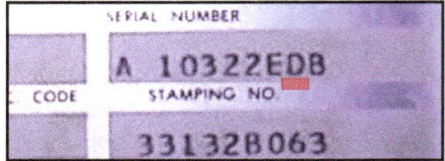

Beginning in the early 1990s, it was the 3rd and 4th number of serial number. There was also a format used for a while that placed the year

A | Serial Number: 4607B20058
BLE FOR OUTDOOR USE
Volts   1   Ph   60   Hz
Minimum Circuit Ampacity

of manufacture at the 7th and 8th digits of the 10-digit sequence that is all numbers. So, for example, serial number 5258470829 would indicate a 2008 year of manufacture.

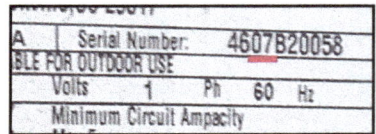

• •

Aspen - First two numbers after an initial letter of serial number are year of manufacture.

MODEL NO.   AEM42B-000+ECL0
SERIAL NO.   L07-00004949

• •

Bard - The 5th and 6th digits of serial number are the year of manufacture for units produced 1980 and later.

SHORT-CIRCUIT CU
BRANCH CIRCUIT SELECT CURRENT 26.3
IAL NUMBER   324L143161680-02
SUITABLE FOR OUTDOOR USE

• •

BDP - The 3rd and 4th numbers of serial number. These are older models of CAC/BDP.

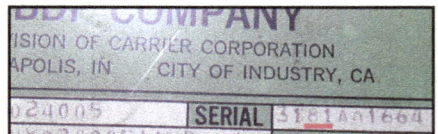

BDP COMPANY
ISION OF CARRIER CORPORATION
APOLIS, IN   CITY OF INDUSTRY, CA
024005   SERIAL 3181AA1664

Bosch - The 1st number in the second grouping of the serial number indicates year but not decade of manufacture. If second number of the 3 letter group is 0, then it is 2010 thru 2013, if a 1 then 2014 thru 2019, and if a 3 then 2020 thru 2025. So 3540-**13**7-TW0008-T111M99991 would be 2021.

Serial Number

S/N : 399A-754-000553-7739832070

• •

Broan - 4th and 5th digits of serial number (after 3 letters) are the year of manufacture.

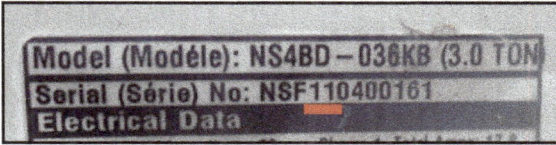

Model (Modéle): NS4BD – 036KB (3.0 TON)
Serial (Série) No: NSF110400161
Electrical Data

• •

Bryant - 3rd and 4th numbers of serial number are the year of manufacture.

SERIA: 3109E03141
PROD 213ANA036000DAA
MODEL 213ANA036-D
METERING TXU   57 PII/GM
DEVICE IN300R   0011003

• •

CAC/BDP - 3rd and 4th number of serial number. These units typically do not a have identifying logo plate. Also, Carrier entered a joint marketing agreement in 2017 with Midea, a Chinese company, to market their HVAC systems with the CAC/BDP name. All serial numbers for these units begin with a "V" and the first two numbers are the year of manufacture.

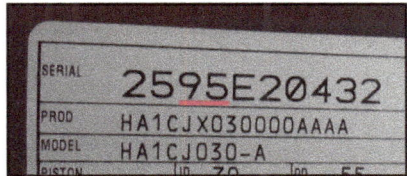

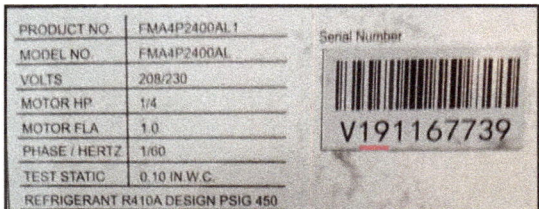

SERIAL 2595E20432
PROD HA1CJX030000AAAA
MODEL HA1CJ030-A
PISTON

PRODUCT NO.	FMA4P2400AL1	Serial Number
MODEL NO.	FMA4P2400AL	
VOLTS	208/230	
MOTOR HP	1/4	
MOTOR FLA	1.0	V191167739
PHASE / HERTZ	1/60	
TEST STATIC	0.10 IN.W.C.	
REFRIGERANT R410A DESIGN PSIG 450		

Carrier - 3rd and 4th numbers of serial number are year of manufacture.

SERIAL NUMBER

2420E11513

PRODUCT NUMBER

• •

Champion - 2nd and 4th digits of serial number are year of manufacture. Manufactured by Unitary Products division of Johnson Controls.

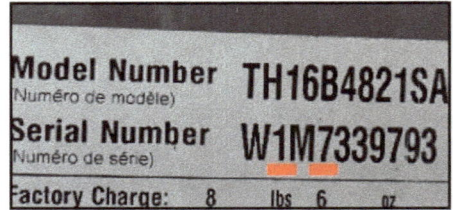

Model Number
(Numéro de modèle)   TH16B4821SA

Serial Number
(Numéro de série)   W1M7339793

Factory Charge: 8   lbs   6   oz

• •

ClimateMaster - If the first digit of the serial number is a letter, then use the letter code system below to determine the year of manufacture.

H = 1998	A = 1999	B = 2000	C = 2001
D = 2002	E = 2003	F = 2004	G = 2005
J = 2006	K = 2007	L = 2008	M = 2009
N = 2010	P = 2011	Q = 2012	R = 2013
S = 2014	T = 2015	U = 2016	V = 2017
W = 2018	X = 2019	Y = 2020	Z = 2021

If the first two digits are numbers, then they are the year of manufacture. This means the unit was built early 1998 or before. So, for example, **94**D142831 was produced in 1994, and **P**122247312 was manufactured in 2011.

• •

Coleman and Coleman-Evcon - There are four variation of the serial number:

1) Used thru 1991, the 3rd and 4th digits are the year of manufacture.

45,200   BTU/HR. BONNET CAPACI

037962003   SERIAL NO.

REMENT: FOR ELEVATION ABOVE 2000 FT DERATE

2) Beginning in 1992, the first two digits of the serial number indicate the age. If the condition of the unit does not make it clear which two numbers are the right ones to use,

look for ANSI or other government standards that the system complies with that have the year of the standard in them.

3 & 4) Coleman-Evcon brand was purchased by York/Unitary Products in 1996 and use either of their two encoding methods. See York info.

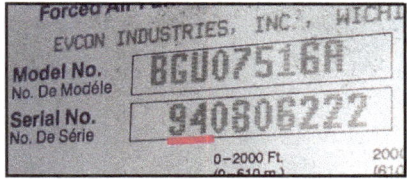

• •

Comfort Pack is manufactured by National Comfort Products. The second and third digits of the serial number are encoded to indicate the year of manufacture, based on the listing below:

32 = late 1998, 33 = 1999, 34 = 2000, 35 = 2001, 36 = 2002, 43 = 2003, 44 = 2005, 46 = 2006, 47 = 2007, 48 = 2008, 49 = 2009, 50 = 2010, 51 = 2011, 52 = 2012, 53 = 2013, 54 = 2014, 55 = 2015, 56 = 2016, 57 = 2017, 58 = 2018, 59 = 2019, 60 = 2020, 61 = 2021, 62 = 2022, 63 = 2023, and so forth.

So, for example, 34**49**21174 would be 2009.

• •

Comfortmaker is manufactured by International Comfort. The first two numbers after a single letter in the serial number are the year of manufacture.

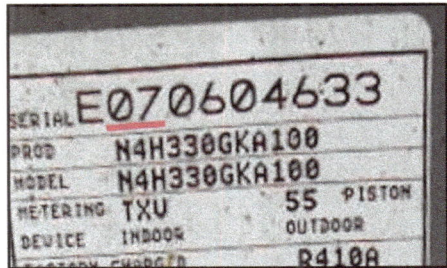

Concord - If there is a single letter in the middle of the serial number, then the 3rd and 4th digits are the year of manufacture, like the example at right. When there is not a letter in the serial

number, then the last two digits at the end of the number are the year, and 0324710591 would mean 1991.

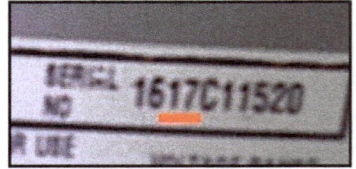

• •

Cumberland was a brand manufactured by American Standard, and followed the Trane/American Standard serial number code format: first letter of serial number indicates year of manufacture. Date of manufacture also listed at upper right. This brand is no longer offered, as far as we know.

T = 1981, U = 1982, W = 1983, X = 1984, Y = 1985, S = 1986, B = 1987, C = 1988, D = 1989, E = 1990, F = 1991, G = 1992, H = 1993, J = 1994, K = 1995, L = 1996, M = 1997, N = 1998,

• •

Daikin - The first two numbers of the serial number are the year of manufacture for a Daikin air conditioner or heat pump. Some units will have the date of manufacture clearly marked in a box on the data plate as "Mfg. Date," and the serial number will not be encoded with the manufacture date.

Daizuki age is not encoded in the serial number. It is simply stated in a "year.month" format near the bottom of the data plate at the side of the unit.

Condenser Fan Motor	0.3A
Minimum Circuit Ampacity	12A
Maximum Over Current Protection	20A
Date of Manufacture	2021.05
OUTDOOR USE UTILISATION À L'EXTÉRIEUR	

• •

Day & Night - the second two digits of the serial number are the year of manufacture.

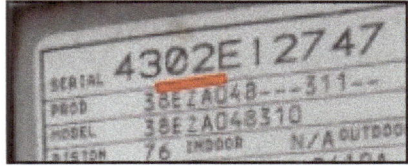

For units from the late 1960s thru the late 1980s, there is a different serial number code, with the single number after an initial letter being the year of manufacture. So the serial number of the unit below indicates it was manufactured in 1978. Because the "8" may be for 1968,1978, or 1988, you want to look at the ANSI certification year, or year of construction of

the home, for guidance. This home was built in 1979, so we determined it that way. Whatever year your figure out, it's a really old system.

• •

Diamond Air - The 3rd and 4th numbers of the serial number are year of manufacture.

• •

Ducane has two formats. They both have 10 digits, but the one you are most likely to encounter will start with four numbers and then a letter. The third and fourth numbers are the year of manufacture. Continued next page...

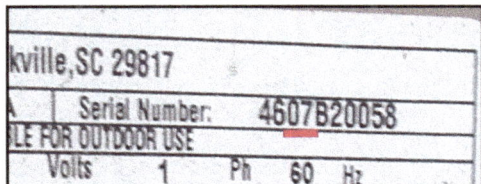

An older format has the year of manufacture at the 7th and 8th digits of the 10-digit sequence that is all numbers.

• •

DuctlessAire - The year of manufacture is at the 12th digit in their long serial number on the condenser data plate. So, be ready to count carefully to locate it. Here's an example: 240132129076**3**290165004 is 2016.

Because these systems were not available in the 2000s, the single digit for the year will not be a problem until we head deeper into the 2020's. Then you will need to check the condition of the outdoor unit, year of certified testing lab approval or industry standard, or year of construction of permit to verify which decade is correct.

• •

EcoTemp is manufactured by International Comfort Products and follows their serial number system. The first two numbers after a single letter are the year of manufacture.

• •

First Co., Aquatherm, and U.S. A/C Products - The first letter of the serial number denotes the year of manufacture, for First Co. products, based on the listing at next page. The serial number may be noted on two lines, as below, or one line. So "I" indicates 2002 manufacture.

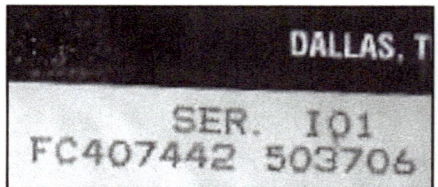

A = 1994/2018, B = 1995/2019, C = 1996/2020, D = 1997/2021
E = 1998/2022, F = 1999/2023, G = 2000/2024, H = 2001/2025
I = 2002/2026, J = 2003/2027, K = 2004/2028, L = 2005/2029
M = 2006/2030, N = 2007, P = 2008, R = 2009, S = 2010
T = 2011, U = 2012, V = 2013, W = 2014, X = 2015, Y = 2016
Z = 2017

Because the alphabetic code is a 24-year repeating cycle, some letters require evaluation of other factors to determine which year is correct.

• •

Florida Heat Pump manufactures geothermal heat pump systems. They have two different serial number systems.
1) For pre-2010 systems, the first letter of the serial number indicates the year of manufacture, starting in alphabetical order with "A" for 1971, but eliminating I, O, and Q, then recycling the letter code over again in 1994.
A = 1971/1994, B = 1972/1995, C = 1973/1996, D = 1974/1997, E = 1975/1998,
F = 1976/1999, F = 1977/2000, G = 1977/2000, H = 1978/2001, J = 1979/2002,
K = 1980/2003, L = 1981/2004, M = 1982/2005, N = 1983/2006, P = 1984/2007
R = 1985/2008, S = 1986/2009, T = 1987, U = 1988, V = 1989, W = 1990,
X = 1991, Y = 1992, Z = 1993

So the first letter of the serial number shown below indicates the heat pump was manufactured 1998, based on the letter "E" and the condition of the unit.

2) For the newer Bosch/FHP units with a longer serial number that begins with a group of four digits, then followed by 3 numbers, the first number of the

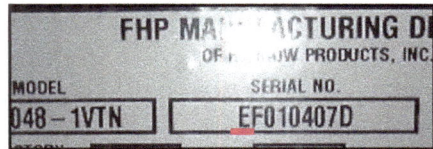

3 letter group is the year—but not the decade—of manufacture. If second number of the 3 letter group is 0, then it is 2010 thru 2013, if a 1 then 2014 thru 2019, and if a 3 then 2020 thru 2025. So 3540-**13**7-TW0008-T111M99991 would be 2021. Yes, it's a little complicated.

Franklin is a brand of inverter-type HVAC system manufactured by Goodman and uses their serial number encoding system. The first two numbers of the serial number are the year of manufacture.

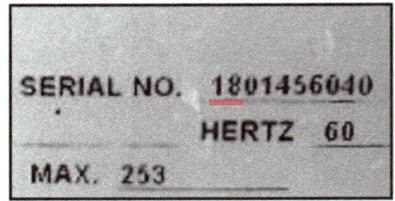

SERIAL NO.   1801456040

HERTZ 60

MAX. 253

• •

Fraser-Johnston - See York.

• •

Fujitsu - Most companies encode the year of manufacture in the serial number, but Fujitsu does not. You can call the Fujitsu Service Department, at (866) 952-8324, with your serial number and they will give you a date.

• •

Frigidaire is a brand manufactured by Nortek (formerly Nordyne) and the fourth and fifth digits of the serial

Model (Modèle):   C3RA–042K

Serial (Série) No: Q3B011001738

number are the year of manufacture for most units. An older format uses five numbers followed by a dash, and then the next two numbers are the year of manufacture. The serial number 31674-95B, for example, was produced in 1995.

• •

Gibson - The 4th and 5th digits of the serial number of are the year of manufacture. So the serial number JSG**14**1118220 indicates 2014. Gibson is manufactured by Nortek.

• •

Goodman - The first two digits of the serial number are the year of manufacture.

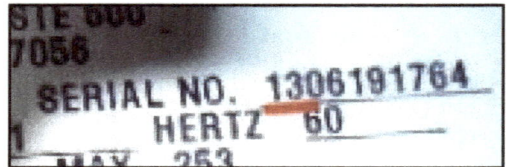

STE 000
7056
SERIAL NO. 1306191764
HERTZ 60

• •

Grandaire - The 4th and 5th digits of serial number are year of manufacture.

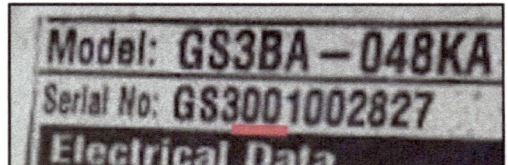

Model: GS3BA – 048KA

Serial No: GS3001002827

Electrical Data

Gree - The third and fourth digits of the serial number are the year of manufacture. Gree also lists the date of manufacture in a year/month format on the data plate.

• •

Guardian is manufactured by Unitary Products Group, and the first two numbers that appear in the serial number (located at the 2nd and 4th digits in the alphanumeric sequence) indicate the year of manufacture.

ZGHGD48S21S1B

Serial No. W1K1290862

• •

Heil is manufactured by International Comfort Products. Units produced since the early 1990s have a serial number that is a single letter followed by a series of numbers. The first two numbers are the year of manufacture.

SERIAL NO.
L913165867

• •

International Comfort Products (ICP) - The first two numbers of the serial number, after a single letter, are the year of manufacture.

SERIAL X131976950
PROD WCH3604GKC100
MODEL WCH3604GKC100

• •

Inter-City Products - The first two numbers in the serial number, after a single letter, are the year of manufacture.

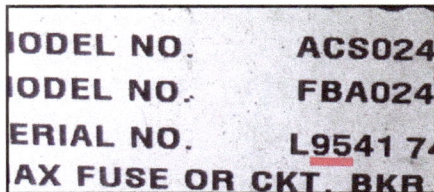

IODEL NO.   ACS024
IODEL NO.   FBA024
ERIAL NO.   L9541 7
AX FUSE OR CKT. BKR

• •

Johnstone is manufactured by Goodman and the first two numbers of the serial number are the year of manufacture.

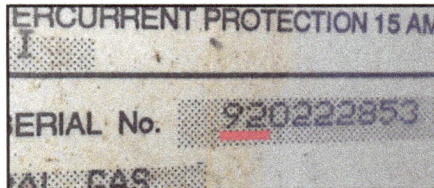

ERCURRENT PROTECTION 15 AM
ERIAL No.   920222853

KeepRite - The first two numbers in the serial number, after a single letter, are the year of manufacture of the unit. If the first digit is not a letter, then the first number is the year of manufacture, but not the decade, which would either be the 1980s or early '90s.

SERIAL	**X131976950**
PROD	WCH3604GKC100
MODEL	WCH3604GKC100
METERING	**TXV**

• •

Kelvinator - The 4th and 5th digits of the serial number are the year of manufacture.

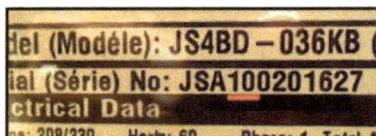

del (Modéle): JS4BD – 036KB
ial (Série) No: JSA100201627
ctrical Data

• •

Kenmore has used multiple different manufacturers over the years to produce HVAC units that they sold under their Kenmore brand. So there is no single recipe for figuring out age from the serial number.

But, if you are pretty sure that the unit was manufactured after 1990, which eliminates earlier mutations, it narrows down to either the first two or second two numbers in serial number as the year of manufacture. There may be a single letter before the numbers, which you can ignore. When you come across a serial number where both sets of numbers are a

SERIAL NO. 9801455542

USE COPPER

possibly correct, you may have to check the condition or ANSI compliance date to see which one is correct.

In the example shown above, it was marked at the bottom of the data plate that the system was manufactured by Goodman, and they go by the first two numbers—so it is 1998. When the data plate references the actual manufacturer you can assume that the serial number complies with their system. Also, if you look carefully around the data plate, the manufacture date is sometimes stated outright, usually in an upper corner.

Lennox - The second two digits of the serial number are the year of manufacture.

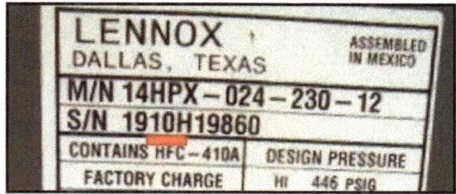

Lennox Minisplit - The year, but not the decade, of manufacture is at the 12th digit in their long serial number on the data plate.

   These units are imported from China and distributed by Lennox in the U.S. They were not available in the 2000s, so the single digit for the year will not be a problem until we head deeper into the 2020's. Then you will need to check the condition of the outdoor unit, year of certified testing lab approval or industry standard, or year of construction of home or remodeling to verify which decade is correct.

· ·

LG - The first digit in the serial number is the year of manufacture, but it does not give you the decade. So, for example, **7**05KWPZ64912 could be 2007 or 2017. Look at the condition of the unit for an indication of the decade. The serial number might also be on a separate sticker below the data plate with a bar code, and include the month and year of manufacture at the end, such as "05 2017."

· ·

Luxaire - See York.

· ·

MagicAire - The first two numbers of the serial number on the data plate, after a single letter, are the year of manufacture. So, for example, W040625437 was manufactured in 2004.

· ·

Magic Chef - See Armstrong.

Magic-Pak package units are designed specifically for multiple-unit buildings. The third and fourth digits in the serial number are the year of manufacture. So 84**12**48427 was produced in 2012.

• •

Maytag - The 4th and 5th digits of the serial number are the year of manufacture.

• •

Midea - The first two numbers after a the letter "V" are the year of manufacture. So the serial number V**19**3157328 indicates production in 2019.

• •

Miller is one the brands manufactured by Nordyne/Nortek, and follows their serial number format. The fourth and fifth digits of the serial number are the year of manufacture.

• •

Mitsubishi - The first digit of the serial number is the last digit of the year. So "6" could be "2006" or "2016," and you will have to look for other clues for the correct decade.

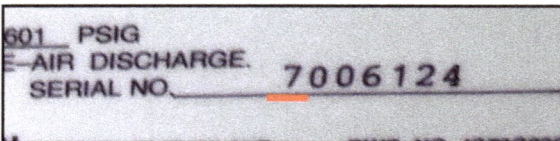

• •

MrCool serial number is 21-digits, and the number at the 12th digit is the year of manufacture. Here's and example: 34076575201**9**3280120410. Because MrCool is a newer brand, a 9 would only mean 2019 for now; but it may evaluating other clues for the decade in years to come.

National Comfort Products is a manufacturer of thru-the-wall HVAC systems for multi-family construction. The second and third digits of the serial number are encoded to indicate the year of manufacture, based on the listing below:
32 = late 1998, 33 = 1999, 34 = 2000, 35 = 2001, 36 = 2002
43 = 2003, 44 = 2005, 46 = 2006, 47 = 2007, 48 = 2008
49 = 2009, 50 = 2010, 51 = 2011, 52 = 2012, 53 = 2013
54 = 2014, 55 = 2015, 56 = 2016, 57 = 2017, 58 = 2018
59 = 2019...and so forth. So, for example, 34**49**21174 would be 2009.

Also, for units built before 9/30/98, the second and third digits after the letter "B" are the actual year of manufacture. So, B**96**214128 is 1996.

• •

Nordyne - The fourth and fifth digits in the serial number are the year of manufacture. Nordyne is the former name of the manufacturer now called Nortek.

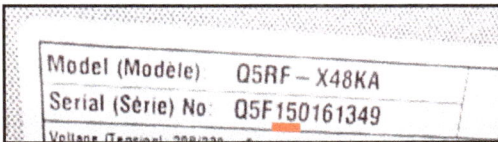

Model (Modèle)	Q5RF – X48KA
Serial (Série) No:	Q5F150161349
Voltage (Tension) 208/230	

• •

Nortek is the new name of the company formerly known as Nordyne. The fourth and fifth characters in the serial number are the year of manufacture.

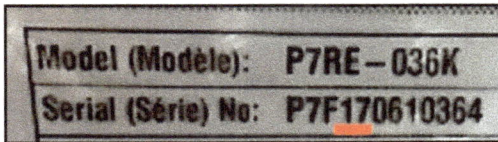

Model (Modèle):	P7RE – 036K
Serial (Série) No:	P7F170610364

• •

Nutone - The fourth and fifth digits of the serial number are the year of manufacture. But there

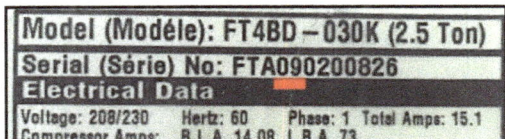

Model (Modéle): FT4BD – 030K (2.5 Ton)
Serial (Série) No: FTA090200826
Electrical Data
Voltage: 208/230   Hertz: 60   Phase: 1 Total Amps: 15.1
Compressor Amps: R L A 14.08 L R A 73

is one exception: if the third digit is not a letter, then the third and fourth digits are the year of manufacture. This only applies to very old ones, most of which are long gone.

Oxbox - The first two numbers in the serial number are the year of manufacture. For example, **21**3251638J would mean manufacture in 2021. Oxbox is a Trane brand.

• •

Panasonic - The age is not encoded in the serial number. It is usually listed on the data plate as "DATE NO." or "PRODUCTION YEAR." For older units, look for a

DATE NO.
2005A
SERIAL NO.
7262100218

letter at the 4th digit of the serial number: J = 1998, K = 1999, N = 2000, R = 2001, T = 2002, W = 2003, X = 2004, R = 2001, T = 2002, W = 2003, X = 2004, Y = 2005.

• •

Pioneer - The date of manufacture is not encoded in the serial number. However, you can call or email them with the serial number and they will look it up in their database and respond with the manufacture date. The serial number is 22-digits long, will be under a bar code and begin with "SN:". Contact them at prwd@pd-hvac.com or (305) 513-4488.

• •

Payne - The third and fourth numbers in the serial number on are the year of manufacture. Newer units will also have the date of manufacture stated at the bottom of the data plate.

• •

Revolv series of HVAC systems by Stylecrest are designed specifically for mobile/manufactured homes. The fourth and fifth characters in the serial number are the year of

Model (Modèle):   RQ7RE – 024K
Serial (Série) No: RQF170581783

manufacture for many systems.

There is also a second serial number system that has a letter at the third digit, and uses the second and fourth digits for the year of manufacture. So W**1**G**2**076523 indicates production in 2012.

Rheem - Find the single letter in the beginning or middle of the serial number. The 3rd and 4th numbers after the letter are the year of manufacture. The month and year of manufacture is also usually indicated at the upper right of the data plate. Then there's the option of going to the Rheem website's serial number lookup page at https://www.rheem.com/how-old-is-my-air-conditioner/.

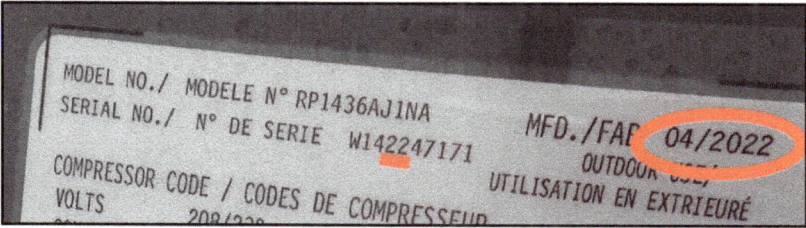

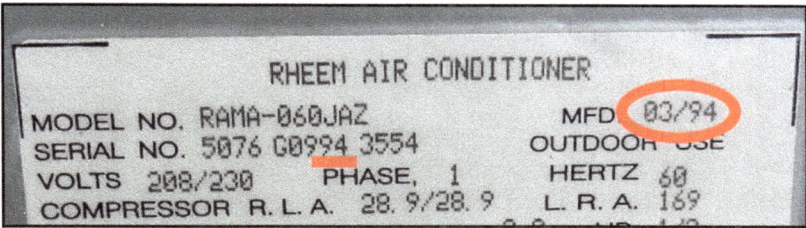

Ruud - See Rheem

RunTru - The year of manufacture is the first two numbers of the serial number on the data plate at the side of the unit, and is also stated at "MFR DATE" at the upper right corner.

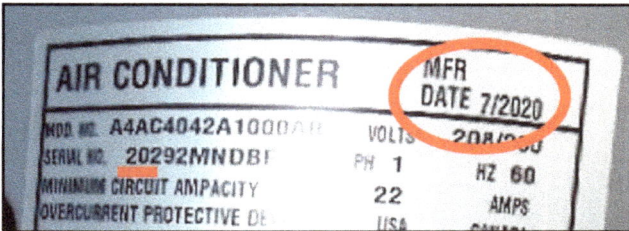

Samsung - See Panasonic.

. . . .

Sanyo - The 6th digit of Sanyo's 7-digit serial number on the data plate is the year of manufacture, but not the decade. So, for example, 024738̲1 could be 1998, 2008, or 2018. Fortunately, the year of manufacture may also be listed directly on the data plate, shown as "Mfr. Date" or "Production Date." If not, then use the condition of the unit to evaluate which decade in which it was manufacted.

. . . .

Sears Kenmore - See Kenmore.

. . . .

Senville - The date of manufacture is not encoded in the serial number. However, you can call or email their tech support department with the serial number and they will look it up in their database and respond with the manufacture date. The serial number is 22-digits long and printed next to the bar code. Contact them at support@senville.com or (800) 242-4935.

. . . .

Tappan is a brand of HVAC equipment that was formerly manufactured by Nortek/Nordyne. The fourth and fifth characters in the serial number are the year of manufacture.

. . . .

Tempstar is manufactured by International Comfort Products, LLC, and the first two numbers in the serial number (after a single letter) are the year of manufacture.

Thermal Zone - The third and fourth numbers after the single letter in the serial number indicate the year of manufacture. It is also noted in the upper right of the manufacturer's data plate.

Trane prints the date of manufacture on all their data plates, usually in the upper right. But, if it is not legible, the age of the unit is also encoded in the first one or two numbers of the serial number.

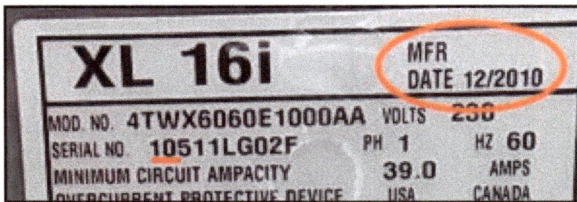

If the first digit of the serial number is a letter:
T = 1981, U = 1982, W = 1983, X = 1984, Y = 1985, S = 1986
B = 1987, C = 1988, D = 1989, E = 1990, F = 1991, G = 1992
H = 1993, J = 1994, K = 1995, L = 1996, M = 1997, N = 1998
P = 1999, R = 2000

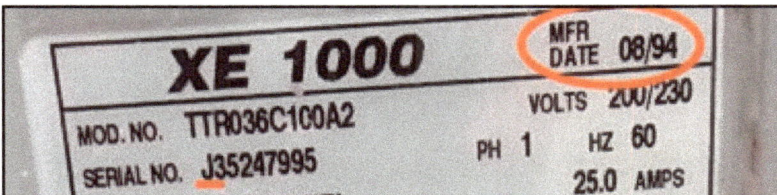

Unitary Products - There are two different serial number formats. Up until 2004, the third letter of the serial number was used to denote year of manufacture by the letter code below:

A = 1971, 1992. B = 1972, 1993, C = 1973, 1994.
D = 1974, 1995, E = 1975, 1996. F = 1976, 1997
G = 1977, 1998. H = 1978, 1999, J = 1979, 2000.
K = 1980, 2001, L = 1981, 2002   M = 1982, 2003
N = 1983, 2004   P = 1984, R = 1985   S = 1986
T = 1987, V = 1988. W = 1989. X = 1990, Y = 1991

So this serial number indicates that it was manufactured in 1996, based on condition of the unit.

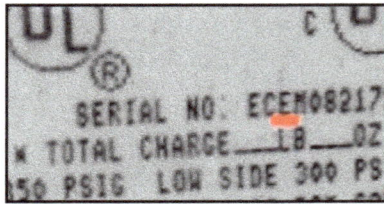

From 2004 to the present, the first two numbers in the serial number, located at the second and fourth characters, are the year of manufacture.

• •

U.S. A/C Products - See First Co.

• •

Weatherking - See Rheem.

• •

Westinghouse - See Nortek/Nordyne.

• •

Xenon - See Goodman.

York - For systems manufactured from October 2004 to the present, the first and third digits in the serial number will be letters, and the second and fourth digits will be numbers that indicate the year of manufacture.

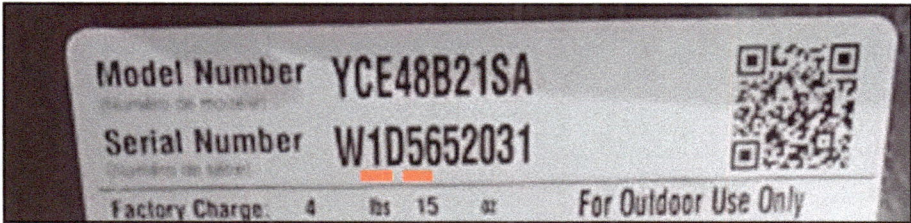

An earlier serial number system, that was used until October 2004, has a sequence of four letters followed by a string of six numbers. The third letter indicates the year of manufacture but, because the letter series repeated every 21 years, some letters will require you to look for other clues for the which age.

A = 1971 or 1992   B = 1972 or 1993, C = 1973 or 1994
D = 1974 or 1995, E = 1975 or 1996   F = 1976 or 1997
G = 1977 or 1998   H = 1978 or 1999, J = 1979 or 2000
K = 1980 or 2001, L = 1981 or 2002   M = 1982 or 2003
N = 1983 or 2004 P = 1984 R = 1985, S = 1986, T = 1987
V - 1988, W = 1989   X = 1990 Y = 1992

So WD<u>H</u>P875237 would be either 1978 or 1999. And here's an example below that could be 1980 or 2001 but, but we also knew that the house was built in 2001—so it is the original system.

GE Zoneline - The second letter of the serial number of a Zoneline PTAC air conditioner or heat pump indicates the year of manufacture, based on a 12-year repeating cycle:

A = 2013, 2001, 1989.   D = 2014, 2002, 1990
F = 2015, 2003, 1991   G = 2016, 2004, 1992
H = 2017, 2005, 1993   L = 2018, 2006, 1994
M = 2019, 2007, 1995   R = 2020, 2008, 1996
S = 2021, 2009, 1997   T = 2022, 2010, 1998
V = 2023, 2011, 1999   Z = 2024, 2012, 2000

So the serial number ARN052A100AC indicates manufacture in 2020, 2008, or 1996. Older models may have fewer digits than this example. To determine which is the correct year, look into the fine print on the data sticker for a compliance standard, such as ASHRAE, which will include the year of the standard. Because manufacturing standards are updated every 3 to 6 years, it will only be near the correct date choice. The condition of the unit provides another hint.

Then again, you might not need to decode the serial number, because the month and year of manufacture may be listed under "MFR DATE/DATE DE FABRICATION" on the data sticker.

How to find age of HVAC system if data plate is missing or not readable

If the data plate on the air conditioner is missing or so faded that it is no longer readable, you already have part of the answer. It's a least 10 years old. But, if you need a more specific age, here's four ways to find it:

1) **Check building permits** - You may be able to get the date of the permit for replacement of the system from your local building department. If they don't have a permit on file, then the unit is either original to the construction of the home or was replaced without a permit. Also, some building departments only keep old permits on file for 10 years, so the permit data may have been discarded.

2) **Check data plate at other half of system** - If it is a split system, and both parts of the system have the same manufacturer and paint color on the cabinet. So check the air handler data plate if the one on the condenser is illegible, or vice-versa.

3) **Ask for homeowner's paperwork** - Many homeowners keep the owner's manual and payment receipt for their system. However, relying on only the homeowner's memory for the age if that's not available can be a mistake. "We just replaced it a few years ago" sometimes turns out be 10 or more after age is verified by another means, especially for seniors.

4) **Condition of condenser** - Condensers (outdoor units) age at different rates according the weather and sun exposure where they are located. But an experienced home inspector can provide an approximate age based on condition. Air handlers are more difficult to age based on condition, but there is usually more than one data plate to check for serial numbers.

Understanding Air Conditioner or Heat Pump Data Plate

There is a lot of information on a condenser data plate that is only important for an air conditioning technician, so here's just what is relevant for the inspector.

1) **Serial Number** - Although the number is only for a particular condenser, the year of manufacture is usually encoded in the front of it, and often the first two or second two numbers are the year of manufacture. For this Carrier heat pump, it is the second two numbers, but varies according to manufacturer, and some of them change their coding over time. Also, there are more complicated systems using letters for the year and a few companies don't encode the year of manufacture in the serial number at all. To learn the serial number format for your brand, enter the brand name in the search bar at the top of this page.

2) **Model Number** - Somewhere in the middle of the model number is a two-digit number that is divisible by 6, and it will tell you the cooling capacity of the unit in tons after conversion from BTU. You need to know that 12,000 BTU equals one ton of air conditioning, which is the measure normally used in the United States. The thousands are dropped off of the number, so 24 equals 2 tons, as at this data plate, and 30 is 2.5 tons, and 60 means 5 tons. You can also use the model or product number to look up more information on the system on the internet.

3) **Factory Charge** - This will tell you whether the system uses the older R-22 refrigerant, which has been phased out, or the current R-410A.

4) **RLA** - The Running Load Amperage is the amount of current in amps that the compressor motor will draw after startup, when operating.

5) **LRA** - The Locked Rotor Amperage is the necessary surge of electricity required to overcome inertia and start up the compressor. This number will be important to you if you plan to run your a/c system using a generator during a power outage. The generator must be able to handle this brief surge of amps, usually 4 or 5 times the RLA.

6) **Max Circuit Breaker or Fuse** - This is always approximately twice the RLA of the compressor. The only time this number becomes a problem is when the system has been changed out for a newer, more energy one, and the breaker for the circuit is not also changed out to a lower amperage rating.

7) **Date of Manufacture** - Sometimes the date of manufacture is directly stated and it is not necessary to decode the serial number. Trane, for example, often places the date of manufacture at the upper right of the data plate.

8) **Heat Pump or Cooling Air Conditioner** - Somewhere near the bottom of the data plate, and often in small letters, it will state whether the condenser is a heat pump (contains a device to reverse the flow of refrigerant from cooling to heating) or a cooling air conditioner (only functions in cooling mode, and usually part of a system with gas furnace).

9) **Name of Manufacturer** - This is often also small letters and may be an acronym. For example, CAC/BDP is a division of the Carrier Corporation.

water
heaters

There are only a handful of manufacturers, such as A.O. Smith and Rheem, that produce most of the water heaters in America under multiple different brand names. If you don't see your brand listed here, look at the fine print on the data plate for the name of the actual manufacturer and use their serial code decoding system.

A.O. Smith - The first two numbers in the serial number, which may appear after one or two letters, are the year of manufacture. This one is 1989

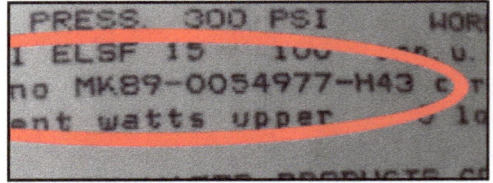

```
PRESS.  300 PSI        HOR
1 ELSF  15      1UU      H. U.
no  MK89-0054977-H43  c T
nt  watts  upper         1c
```

A.O. Smith tankless - The first two numbers of the serial number on the data plate are the year of manufacture. Shown is 2015.

```
NO.  AT-1155-DV-N
No. 1 5 9 0 0 0 6 4 6
Gas ▭           NATUI
```

American - The first two numbers of the serial number are the year of manufacture. The one at the right is 2004.

```
RIAL
MBER 0452121925
YEAR WEEK
```

American ProLine - The first two numbers of the serial number are the year of manufacture. Shown is 2000.

```
G61      18T04    2N
       0037107054
```

Ariston - Ariston has a rather long and complicated serial number system. But, the short version of it is that the 10th and 11th digits of the serial number are the year of manufacture. The number 3605034/35/**08**/133/30055097, for example, indicates- a manufacture date of 2008.

Bosch tankless - The first two numbers in the serial number are encoded to give you the year of manufacture for water heaters before 2010. The first number is the year of manufacture, and the second number is the decade encoded, with 6 = 1990s and 8 = 2000s. So **58**5012459 is 2005, and FB**76**009742 is 1997. The actual date of manufacture is clearly stated on the data plate beginning in 2010.

. . . .

Bradford White - They use a 20-letter code for the year of manufacture of their water heaters. The first letter of the serial number is the one to

```
200 ... ...ITE CORPORATION
              ...    MIDDLEVIL
    ... No: MI40T6EN1...
Serial No: YD1155948  ...sh No
       40(...
Input: 40000        (Btu/hr.) ...
```

use. The letters I, O, Q, R, U and V are excluded. Because the letter code recycles every 20 years "A," for example, can be 1964, 1984, 2004. You have to use your own judgement of the condition of the water heater to determine which year is correct. Knowing when the house was built is also helpful.

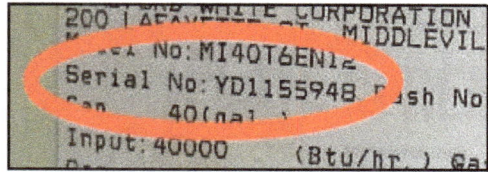

A = 1964, 1984, 2004   B = 1965, 1985, 2005
C = 1966, 1986, 2006   D = 1967, 1987, 2007
E = 1968, 1988, 2008   F = 1969, 1989, 2009
G = 1970, 1990, 2010   H = 1971, 1991, 201
J = 1972, 1992, 2012   K = 1973, 1993, 2013
L = 1974, 1994, 2014   M = 1975, 1995, 2015
N = 1976, 1996, 2016   P = 1977, 1997, 2017
S = 1978, 1998, 1998   T = 1979, 1999, 2019
W = 1980, 2000, 2020   X = 1981, 2001, 2021
Y = 1982, 2002, 2022   Z = 1983, 2003, 2023

. . . .

US Craftmaster - The first two numbers of the serial number are the year of manufacture. Shown is 2013.

```
         ...
SERIAL
NUMBER   1332T460473
```

Eccotemp tankless - The first two numbers of the serial number are the year of manufacture. So the serial number ECC**20**290387 means the unit was produced in 2020.

· ·

EcoSmart - The third and fourth digits of the Date Code are the year of manufacture. This unit was manufactured in 2021.

· ·

Eemax tankless - The first two numbers of the serial number are the year of manufacture. Shown is 2015.

· ·

Env-Ro-Temp - The first two numbers of the serial number are the year of manufacture. Be sure to not confuse the product number with the serial number. This unit is 1998.

· ·

GE - The third and fourth numbers (after the letters) in the serial number are the year of manufacture. Newer water heaters will also list the date of manufacture directly. Shown is 2001.

· ·

GSW - The first two numbers in the serial number are the year of manufacture. For example, a serial number U**13**10372185 means that the water heater was manufactured in 2013.

Insinkerator instant water heater - The first two numbers in the serial number are the year of manufacture. Shown is 2012.

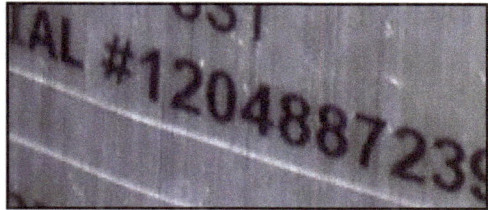

. . . .

Intertherm - The third and fourth numbers in the serial number are the year of manufacture. This one is 1985.

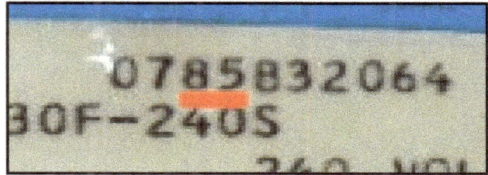

. . . .

Jackson - Most Jackson water heaters we have come across do not encode the date of manufacture in the serial number. The date appears at the address line at top of the data plate. Pictured to the right is April 1978.

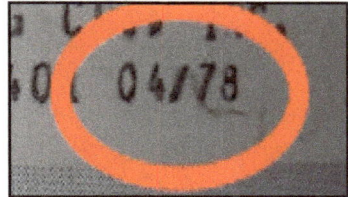

However, some units encoded the month and year in the last 4 digits of the serial number, with the last two digits being the year. So the example on the bottom was manufactured in 1979.

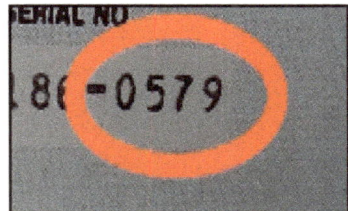

. . . .

Jacuzzi tankless - The first letter of the serial number indicates the year of manufacture. This example is 2014.

A = 2009, B = 2010, C = 2011, D = 2012, E = 2013, F = 2014
G = 2015, H = 2016, J = 2017, K = 2018, L = 2019, M = 2020
N = 2021, P = 2022, R = 2023, S = 2024, T = 2025,
W = 2026, X = 2027, Y = 2028, Z = 2029

John Wood - The first two numbers of the serial number, after a single letter, are the year of manufacture. So, for example, S**11**12F601242 would mean it was produced in 2011.

. . . .

water heaters

Kenmore - The first two numbers in the serial number are the year of manufacture. To the right is 1987 and below it is 2012.

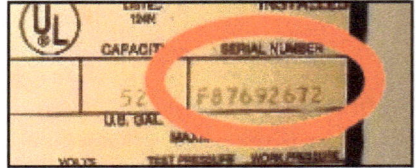

. . . .

Marey - The first four digits of the serial number are the year of manufacture. The unit pictured is 2016.

2016.12 MHI026-16.16807

. . . .

Maytag - The first two numbers of the serial number (after a single letter) are the year of manufacture. Shown is 2000.

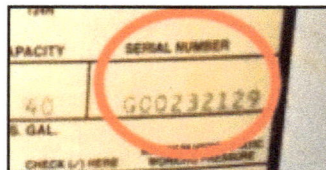

. . . .

Mor-Flo - The first two numbers of the serial number are the year of manufacture. This one is 1998.

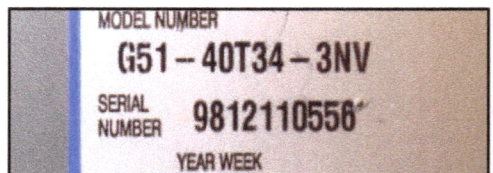

Navien - Look for the number between two letters in the middle of the serial number. For example, the "14" between "C" and "X" in the data tag shown above indicates the water heater was manufactured in 2014.

A older serial number system specifies the year of manufacture in the second group of numbers in a sequence of three or four groups. For example, the serial number 98881-**2010**0505-3026 translates to 2010 year of manufacture.

water heaters

• •

Noritz - The first four digits of the serial number are the year of manufacture. This is 2006.

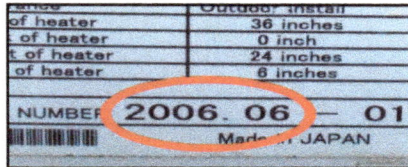

• •

Paloma tankless - The third and fourth numbers of the serial number on the data plate, after several letters, are the year of manufacture. Shown is 2007.

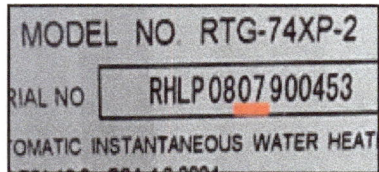

• •

Premier Plus - The first two numbers of the serial number are the year of manufacture for a Premier Plus water heater. So the data plate shown indicates that the water heater was manufactured in 2005.

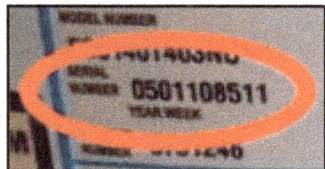

Reliance - The first two numbers (after a single letter) of the serial number are the year of manufacture of Reliance water heaters. So the water heater with the data plate shown is from 1995.

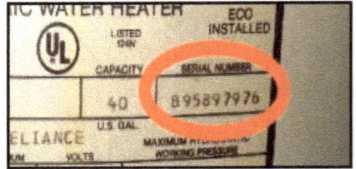

• •

Rheem - The third and fourth numbers in the serial number, usually after several letters, is the year of manufacture. So the data plate indicates that it was made in 2001.

• •

Rheem tankless - The third and fourth numbers, after a single letter, are the year of manufacture. So the data plate of the water heater shown was manufactured in 2015.

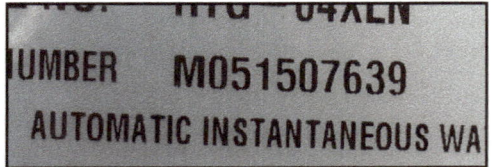

• •

Richmond - Richmond water heaters are manufactured by Rheem, and the 3rd and 4th numbers of the serial number are the year of manufacture. So the data plate shown indicates the water heater was manufactured in 2001.

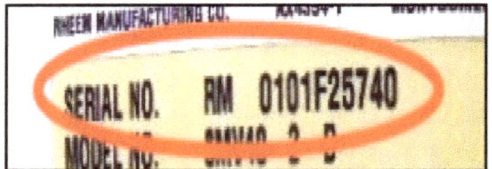

• •

Rinnai - There are two different formats for a Rinnai serial number. The first one was used until mid-2009, with an example shown at right. The first two digits are the year of manufacture. The manufacture date may also be stated after the serial number.

In late 2009, it was switched to a letter-code, with first letter of the serial number being the year
A = 2009, B = 2010, C = 2011,
D = 2012, E = 2013, F = 2014,
G = 2015, H = 2016, J = 2017,
K = 2018, L = 2019, M = 2020

So the serial number indicates the water heater was manufactured in 2013.

• •

Ruud - The third and fourth numbers in the serial number, usually after several letters, is the year of manufacture. So the manufacture year is 1985.

• •

Seisco tankless- The first two numbers of the serial number are the year of manufacture. This water heater was produced in 2015.

• •

SioGreen tankless - Most brands of water heaters have the year of manufacture encoded in the serial number, but SioGreen does not. You have to call their tech support line at **(888) 270-8452** with the serial number, and they will provide a manufacture date.

• •

State Industries - The first two numbers of the serial number of a State water heater are the year of manufacture. Newer State water heaters, like the one shown from 2013 also list the "BUILD DATE" below the serial number so there's no interpretation necessary; but, for older ones, you will have to depend on the serial number.

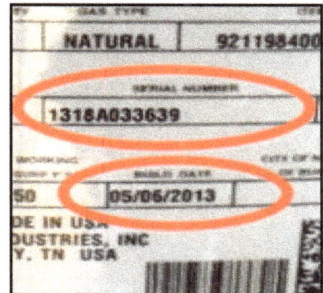

Stiebel Eltron - Look at the middle cluster of four digits in the serial number. Add 25 to the first two digits for the year of manufacture.

No.: 222423-8965-025836

| Heat pump

So the heat pump water heater with the serial number shown was manufactured in 2014.

. . . .

Takagi - The first two numbers of the serial number are the year of manufacture, so the serial number shown

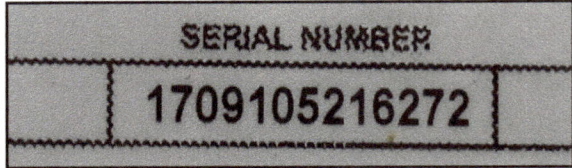

SERIAL NUMBER

1709105216272

means the water heater was manufactured in 2017.

. . . .

Tempra tankless - Tempra tankless water heaters are manufactured by Stiebel Eltron and follow the same serial number format for determining their age

239215-9453-900611

h TO 300 psi / 20 bar / 2 M

as the company's tank-type water heaters. Look at the middle cluster of four digits in the serial number. Add 25 to the first two digits for the year of manufacture. This one was manufactured in 2019.

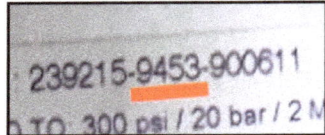

. . . .

Therm-a-flow - The first two digits of the serial number on the data plate are the year of manufacture of a Therm-a-flow water heater, which is manufactured by Mor-Flo. The example was produced in 1983.

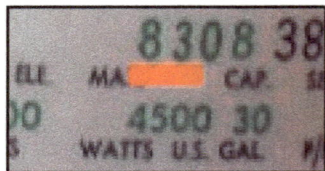

8308 38

ELE   MA   CAP

0   4500 30

WATTS U.S. GAL

. . . .

Tiny Titan - The first two numbers of the serial number are the year of manufacture, so the serial number shown on the next page indicates the water heater was manufactured in 2015. Tiny

water heaters

Titan is a line of small-tank (2.5 to 20 gal) water heater produced by American Water Heater. It should not be confused with Titan tankless water heaters, manufactured by Niagara Industries.

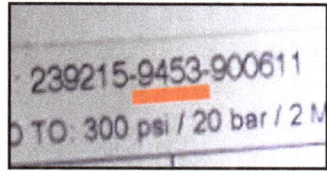

• •

Titan tankless - Look for a sticker at the bottom of the water heater that says "Date of Manufacture (DOM)," which will state it in a month/day/year format. If the

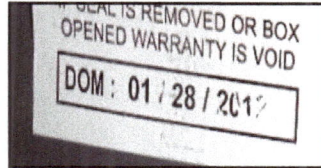

sticker is missing you can call the manufacturer, Niagara Industries at (305) 876-9010, with the serial number and they will give you the production date.

The Titan electric tankless water heater should not be confused with the Tiny Titan brand, a small tank-type water heater designed for under-counter installation and produced by American Water Heater.

• •

Thermalux tankless - The Thermalux serial number is 12 digits, and the first four digits are the year of manufacture, followed by a period. So the serial number **2020**.10-043012 means the unit was manufactured in October, 2020.

• •

Triangle Tube - Although many manufacturers encode the date of manufacture in their serial number, Triangle Tube does not. The year of manufacture may be found on data plate of some units but, If not, you need to call their tech support line at **(856) 228-8881**, extension 575, with your serial number and they will look up the age for you.

water heaters

US Craftmaster - The first two numbers of the serial number are the year of manufacture for a US Craftmaster water heater, so the data plate indicates it was manufactured in 2013

MODEL NUMBER
E2F30LD035V
SERIAL NUMBER 1332T460473

• •

Westinghouse - The 5th and 6th digits of the serial number are the year of manufacture of a Westinghouse water heater. So 0215**18**H2008455 indicates the water heater was manufactured in 2018. Newer units also have the date listed near the serial number.

MODEL WEC080C2X045
SERIAL 021518H2008455

• •

Whirlpool - Whirlpool water heaters are manufactured by Craftmaster, and their coding system is that the first two numbers of the serial number are the year of manufacture. So the serial number of the water heater data plate in the photo indicates that the water heater was manufactured in 2005.

E1F50RD045V
SERIAL NUMBER 0511131187
PRODUCT 0826230

electrical panels

There is often a serial number code or date code on a data sticker inside the panel door or panel box interior of the load center. Sometimes it's just stamped on the box itself. Each manufacturer has their own code and some of them, like Square D, have changed their encoding system over the years. Here are the brands of panels that we have info about determining their age.

Bryant - We do not know of any markings on the panel box or data sticker that indicate date of manufacture. But it became a division of Westinghouse in the 1901, and Westinghouse ceased production of Bryant brands panels in 1988. So any panels still installed are at pushing 40-years of age, and likely much older.

· ·

electrical panels

Challenger - The first two numbers in a stamp at the wiring diagram on the door of a Challenger panel are the week of manufacture, and the third digit is the year. This does not tell you which decade, which will

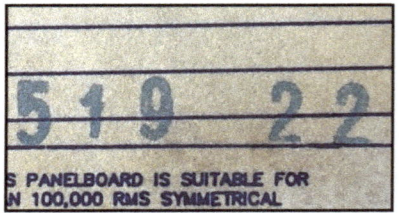

have to be determined from other clues. The example above was in a house built in 1990, so we were able to determine a 1989 production date.

Challenger panels were produced from the mid-1970s until 1994. They have had multiple manufacturer recalls, and many insurance companies will not accept them.

· ·

Cutler-Hammer - load centers use a five-digit date code that's at the bottom of the data sticker inside the box at the side. First digit identifies which plant manufactured it, second digit is the year, third and fourth digits are the week, and last digit is a code for the decade. So the second and final digits are the ones you want to look for. To decode the last digit:
+ is 1980 – 1989,   = is 1990 – 1999,   & is 2000 – 2009
! is 2010 – 2019,   @ is 2020 – 2029,   # is 2030 – 2039
$ is 2040 – 2049

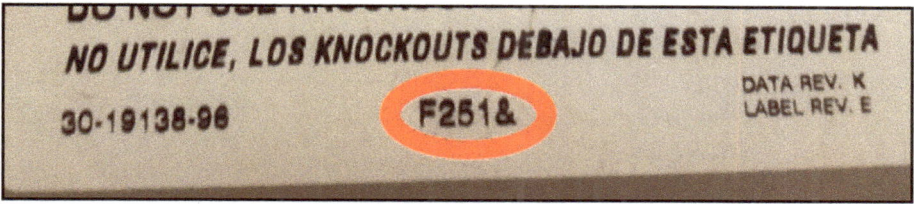

NO UTILICE, LOS KNOCKOUTS DEBAJO DE ESTA ETIQUETA

30-19138-96   F251&   DATA REV. K
                                    LABEL REV. E

So the F251& code shown above means that it was manufactured in 2002 (2nd year of the 2000 to 2009 decade), on the 51st week. The code is in very small type and turned sideways.

. . . .

Eaton uses the same date code as Cutler-Hammer. So the **F618!** code shown below means that it was manufactured in 2016 (sixth year of the 2010 to 2019 decade), on the 18th week.

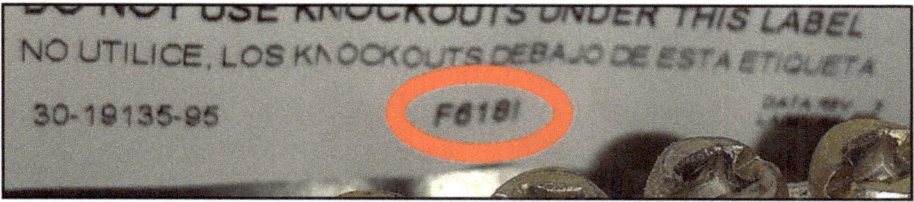

NO UTILICE, LOS KNOCKOUTS DEBAJO DE ESTA ETIQUETA

30-19135-95   F618!

. . . .

Federal Pacific - These panels were manufactured from the 1950s to 1985, so most of them are 50+ years old. No serial number decoding available. Because of a safety defect in the panel design, they are not acceptable to most insurance companies.

. . . .

GE load centers have an eight-digit serial number of two letters followed by six numbers, and the second letter indicates the year of manufacture, based on a repeating 12-year cycle. The serial number is

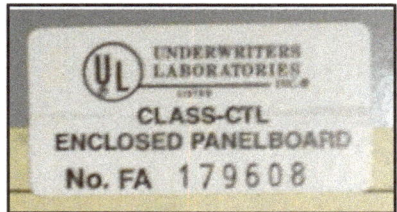

UNDERWRITERS LABORATORIES
CLASS-CTL
ENCLOSED PANELBOARD
No. FA 179608

usually located on a small sticker on, or near, the wiring diagram on the inside of the panel door.
A = 2013, 2001, 1989, 1977, 1944
B = 1945,   C = 1946
D = 2014, 2002, 1990, 1978, 1947

E = 1969, 1948
F = 2015, 2003, 1991, 1979, 1949
G = 2016, 2004, 1992, 1980, 1950
H = 2017, 2005, 1993, 1981, 1951
J = 1952, K = 1953
L = 2018, 2006, 1994, 1982, 1970, 1954
M = 2019, 2007, 1995, 1983, 1971, 1955
N = 1972, 1956, P = 1973, 1957
R = 2020, 2008, 1996, 1984, 1972, 1958
S = 2021, 2009, 1997, 1984, 1973, 1959
T = 2010, 1998, 1986, 1974, 1960
V = 2011, 1999, 1987, 1975
Z = 2012, 2000, 1988, 1976

Between 19961 and 1968 they used three letters at the be-ginning of the serial number, and the second and third letters indicated the year.

VU = 1961, WV = 1962, XW = 1963, YX = 1964, AY = 1965, BZ = 1966, CA = 1967, DB = 1968

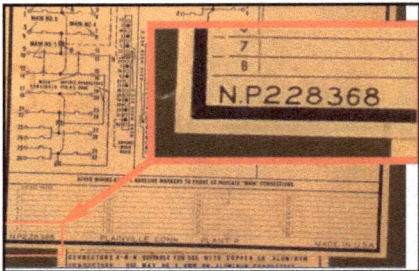

Yes, this makes it complicated to figure out which year is the correct one. Knowing the year of the original construction of the house or any major remodeling may help you get closer to the right one. Here's an example below of an older panel that has the serial number at the bottom of the wiring diagram.

• •

Gould - Some panels have a stamp on the wiring diagram sticker, and the last two digits are the year of manufacture. So the two shown below were manufactured in 1977 and 1983. Also, some panels do not have this stamp.

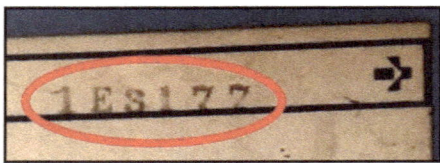

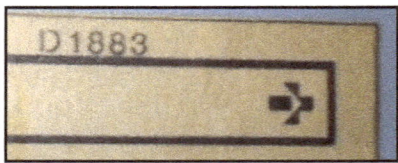

Any panel with the Gould name on it is already really old. And a bit of corporate history will give you a loose time frame: Gould merged with ITE in 1976, and their panels were rebranded as ITE-Gould shortly afterwards. Then Siemens gobbled up ITE-Gould in 1983 and phased out the brand over the next few years. So any panel with the Gould name on it is already really old.

. . . .

ITE - look for a 5-digit date code of a single letter followed by four numbers. The last two digits are the year of manufacture, and the 1st digit is the month, encoded as: A = January, B = February, C = March, D = April, E = May, F = June, G = July, H = August, J = September, K = October, L = November, and M = December. The 2nd and 3rd digits are day of the month. You can find the code stamped on the wiring diagram sticker on the inside of the panel door. Hopefully it's still intact all these years later. So, for example, **B2685** (shown below) was produced on February 26, 1985.

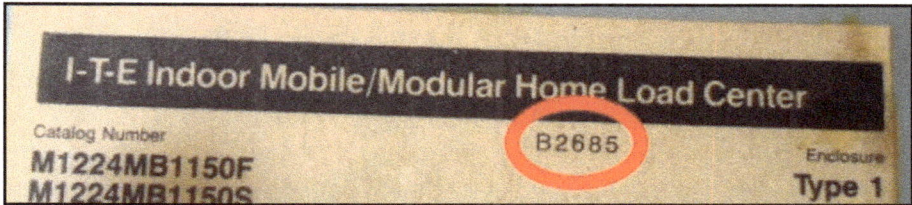

Gould acquired ITE in 1976 and, between 1976 and 1983, the panels were branded as "ITE Gould." Then Siemens gobbled up Gould ITE in 1983, retired the name shortly after, and transitioned to their date system over the next few years, with some overlap between the two. See Siemens for that date

. . . .

Murray - The date of manufacture of newer panels—the ones produced since Siemens took over the brand in the 1990s—can be found at the bottom of the paper data plate on the inside of the panel door, as shown in the example above. But Murray

Electrical was founded way back in 1899 and went through several changes of ownership before Siemens took over, including by Arrow Hart and Crouse Hinds in the 1970s. We are not familiar with how to determine the age of the older Murray panel boards. Siemens stopped producing Murray brand panels in 2019, but the panel design is compatible with Siemens circuit breakers.

. . . .

Pushmatic breakers were first produced in the late 1930s, but most panels and breakers date from the late 1940s through 1970, although manufactured up until the mid-1980s. But we have never seen a Pushmatic panel in a home built after the '60s. So any panel still around is a minimum of 50 years old, and probably much more. No known date code.

. . . .

Siemens - most load centers have the date of manufacture stamped in ink on the back of the panel box near the bottom as shown at right. In some panels, the date may be embossed in the metal instead of stamped in ink. The date may be partially concealed by wiring in the panel.

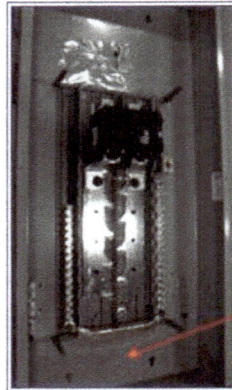
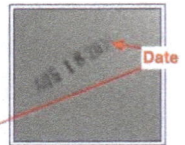

Date

Siemens panels from the 1980s to early '90s may have a small stamp near the top of the data sticker, like this one from 1988.

SIEMENS

ured Housing Load Cent

B2688

Also, some newer Siemens panels have the manufacture date stamped on the data sticker on the inside of the panel door, like in the photo below.

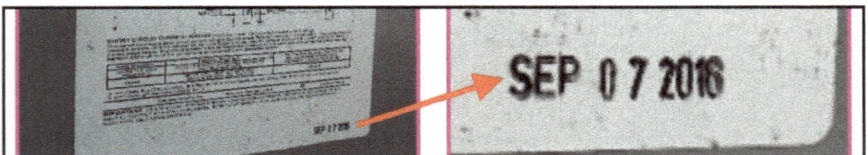

SEP 07 2016

Square D -The alpha-numeric sequence is usually a stamp over the wiring diagram, as shown in the photo above. It would be more accurately described as a date-code system, since each panel box does not have a unique number. The diagram below is for panel manufactured from 1956 to approximately 2002.

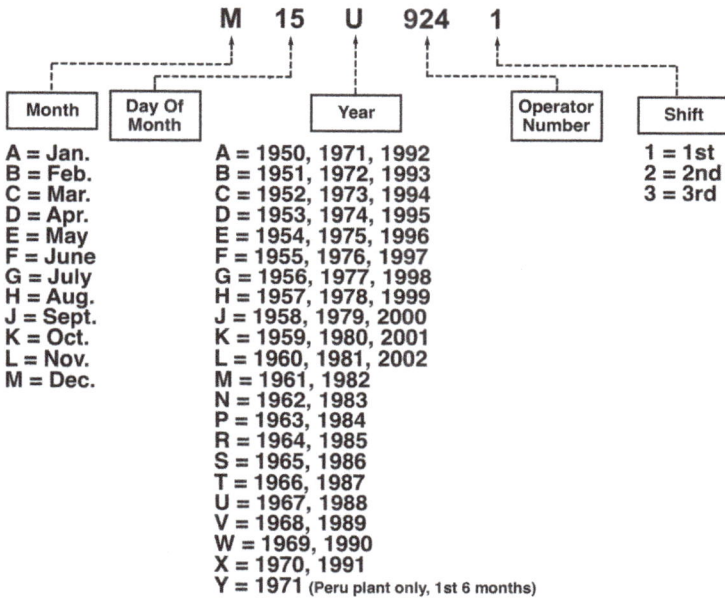

M   15   U   924   1

Month	Day Of Month	Year	Operator Number	Shift

Month	Year	Shift
A = Jan.	A = 1950, 1971, 1992	1 = 1st
B = Feb.	B = 1951, 1972, 1993	2 = 2nd
C = Mar.	C = 1952, 1973, 1994	3 = 3rd
D = Apr.	D = 1953, 1974, 1995	
E = May	E = 1954, 1975, 1996	
F = June	F = 1955, 1976, 1997	
G = July	G = 1956, 1977, 1998	
H = Aug.	H = 1957, 1978, 1999	
J = Sept.	J = 1958, 1979, 2000	
K = Oct.	K = 1959, 1980, 2001	
L = Nov.	L = 1960, 1981, 2002	
M = Dec.	M = 1961, 1982	
	N = 1962, 1983	
	P = 1963, 1984	
	R = 1964, 1985	
	S = 1965, 1986	
	T = 1966, 1987	
	U = 1967, 1988	
	V = 1968, 1989	
	W = 1969, 1990	
	X = 1970, 1991	
	Y = 1971 (Peru plant only, 1st 6 months)	

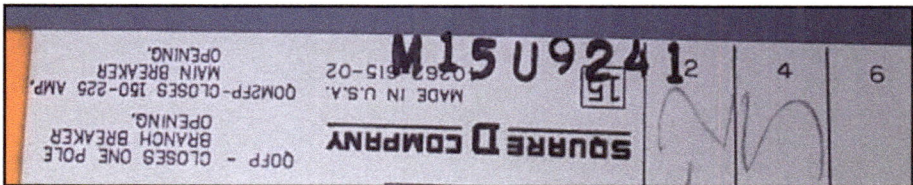

So the date-code shown above indicates that the panel was manufactured on December 15th of 1967 or 1988, by operator #924, on the first shift. Since the letter indicating year of manufacture can be one of several that are 21-years apart, you should evaluate the condition of the panel to determine which one that is most likely correct. Year of construction of the home, along with the year of any remodeling or electrical upgrades can further clarify it.

Here's another example, below, that was manufactured on September 29th of 1952, 1973, or 1994, by operator #462, on the first shift. In this case, since we knew that the home was built in

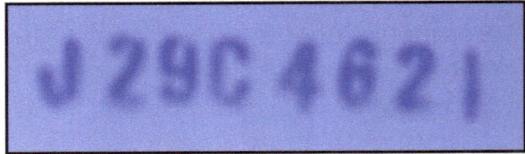

1995, it was easy to establish that 1994 was the year of manufacture.

Panels from the late 1990s until the present most commonly use a five or six digit code, where the first two digits are the year, second two digits are the week. So "991731" would have been manufactured in 1999, on the 17th week of the year.

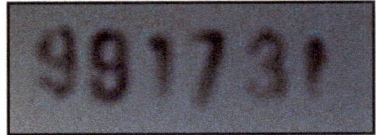

. . . .

electrical panels

Thomas & Betts - Some panelboards have a year/month/day stamp on the data sticker at the inside of the panel door, but others do not. Since they were only produced between 1994 and 2003, that narrows it down considerably, even without a date stamp.

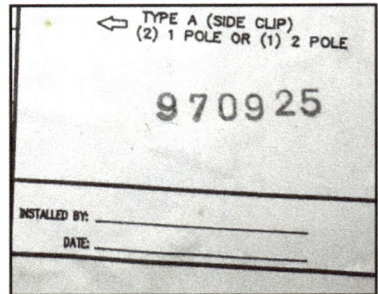

. . . .

Walker Electrical Company was founded by Ralph Walker in 1939 in Atlanta, Georgia. It was absorbed by I-T-E sometime in the 1950s, and then I-T-E itself went through several mergers beginning in

1968, and was eventually acquired by Siemens. The Walker brand appears to have been abandoned in the late 1960s, so any panel with a Walker nameplate is at least 60 years old. The photo above was from an original panel installed in a 1963 home. Unfortunately, we know of no serial number to decode for the exact age

Wadsworth Electrical Manufacturing Company dates back to1918, and was most popular from the 1930s to 1950s. The company liquidated in 1990, but sales of their electrical equipment gradually deteriorated from the '70s onward, and we have not seen any Wadsworth panels installed in homes after the early-1970s. Sothat makes most Wadsworth panels still installed at least 50 years old. We know of no serial number to decode for the exact age.

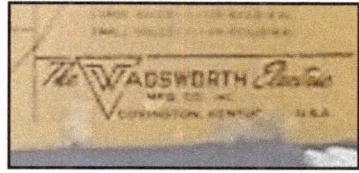

. . . .

Westinghouse - The third number of the serial number stamped on the data sticker of the panel is the single-digit year of manufacture, and the first two numbers are the week. Because the decade is not provided, it must be figured out from other observations.

This panel was in a mobile home built in February of 1990, and that's how we determined that it was 1989. Because production of Westinghouse panels was discontinued in 1995, the manufacture date must be earlier than that.

Not all Westinghouse panels will have this number stamp. Some have a letter sequence that we have been unable to decipher.

. . . .

If the data sticker is missing, there is no serial number, or the serial number is not decipherable, there are still several ways to get the approximate age of a panel:

1) For brands that are no longer manufactured, the timespan when they were in production will get you closer to the age. Tomas & Betts, for example, was manufactured from the 1994 to 2003.

2) The year of construction of the house is often also the age of the panel. Or any permits for additions or remodeling are a likely time for panel replacement.

3) Any building permits for a service upgrade or panel replacement will also provide a panel age.

electrical panels

life expectancy

APPLIANCES

Clothes Dryer, Gas or Electric - 10 to 16 years, average 14
Dishwasher - 6 to 15 years, average 10
Electric Range - 13 to 18 years, average 15
Freezer - 12 to 20 years, average 16
Garbage Disposal - 10 to 14 years, average 12
Gas Range - 15 to 22 years, average 18
Microwave Oven - 6 to 9 years, average 8
Refrigerator, Full Size - 10 to 18 years, average 14
Refrigerator, Compact - 6 to 12 years, average 8
Washing Machine - 9 to 16 years, average 12

CABINETS and SHELVES

Bathroom Cabinets - 30 to 60 years, average 50
Kitchen Cabinets - 30 to 60 years, average 45
Medicine Cabinets - 30+ years
Closet and Pantry Shelves - 40 to 100+ years, average 70

DOORS

Exterior
Fiberglass, Exterior - 50 to 100+ years, average 70
Garage Doors - 20 to 35 years, average 30
Garage Door Openers - 10 to 15+ years, average 12
Screen Door, Wood or Vinyl, 20 to 30 years, average 25
Sliding Glass - 20 to 30 years, average 25
Steel, Exterior - 30 to 80+, average 50
Wood, Exterior - 40 to 100+ years, average 70

Interior
Closet - 30 to 100+ years, average 50
Wood French, Interior - 40 to 70 years, average 50
Wood, Interior Hollow Core - 30 to 50+ years, average 40
Wood, Interior Solid Core - 50 to 100+ years, average 70

life expectancy

ELECTRICAL

Panel - 50+ years
Circuit Breaker - 30 to 40 years, average 35
AFCI or CAFCI Circuit Breaker - 30 to 40 years, average 35
GFCI Circuit Breaker - 30 to 40 years, average 35
GFCI Receptacle Outlet - 15 to 25 years, average 20
Light Fixture, Exterior - 25 to 45 years, average 35
Light Fixture, Interior - 40 to 50 years, average 45
Wall Switch - 30 to 40 years, average 35
Receptacle Outlet - 50+ years
Wire Metal - 100+ years
Wire Insulation - 50 to 80 years, average 70
Whole-House Generator - 10 to 20 years, average12
Whole-House Surge Protector - 2 to 5 years, average 3

FOUNDATIONS

Concrete Footing - 100+ years
Concrete Piers and Grade Beam - 70 to 100 years, average 80
Concrete or Brick Pier on Grade - 50 to 80 years, average 65
Stacked Concrete Block on Pad (mobile home) - 25 to 50 years, average 40
Thickened Edge Concrete Slab - 100+ years
Treated or Cypress Wood Piles - 40 to 75 years, average 60

FLOOR and ROOF WOOD STRUCTURE

Roof Truss - 100+ years
Floor Truss - 100+ years
Roof Sheathing - 100+ years

life expectancy

HEATING, VENTILATION and AIR CONDITIONING (HVAC)

Attic Fan - 5 to 15 years, average 10
Bathroom Exhaust Fan - 9 to 12 years, average 10
Ceiling Fan - 6 to 10 years, average 8
Ductless (mini-split) - 10 to 16 years, average 14
Ducts - 25 to 70 years, average 45
Electric Furnace - 18 to 24 years, average 21
Gas Furnace - 15 to 22 years, average 19
Kitchen Exhaust or Range Hood Fan - 12 to 18 years, average 15
Package Unit - 10 to 16 years, average 14
Split System Condenser (outside unit) - 10 to 16 years, average 14
Split System Air Handler (inside unit) - 14 to 18 years, average 17
Thermostat - 10 to 25 years, average 15 years
Whole House Attic Fan - 10 to 20 years, average 16

PAINT and CAULK

Paint, Exterior - 7 to 10 years
Paint, Interior - 10 to 15 years
Caulk, Exterior - 7 to 10 years
Caulk, Interior - 7 to 15 years

life expectancy

PLUMBING PIPE

ABS (Acrylonitrile Butadiene Styrene) - 50 to 80 years, average 70
Cast Iron - 50 to 70 years, average 60
Copper - 50 to 80 years, average 70
CPVC (Chlorinated Polyvinyl Chloride) - 50 to 80 years, average 70
Galvanized Steel - 40 to 60 years, average 50
Orangeburg (bituminous fiber) - 50 years
PB (PolyButylene) - 10 to 20 years, average 12, no longer code approved or manufactured due premature failure problems
PEX (Cross-linked Polyethylene) - 40 to 50 years, average 45
PVC (Polyvinyl Chloride) - 50 to 80 years, average 70

PLUMBING FIXTURES

Bathtub - 10 to 50 years, average 25
Faucets - 15 to 25 years, average 20
Fiberglass Tub/Shower - 10 to 20 years, average 15
Hose Bibb - 15 to 25 years, average 20
Hose Bibb Vacuum Breaker - 5 to 12 years, average 7
Shower Pan Liners - 40 to 50 years, average 45
Shut-off Valves - 10 to 25 years, average 20
Sinks - 15 to 100+ years, average 30
Toilets, Bidets, Urinals - 20 to 100 years, average 50
Toilet Tank Components - 5 to 10 years, average 7
Water Heater, Tank - 10 to 20 years, average 12
Water Heater, Tankless - 20 years

ROOF SYSTEMS

Asbestos Cement Shingles - 40 to 60 years, average 50
Asphalt Shingles, 3-Tab - 16 to 22 years, average 20
Asphalt Shingles, Architectural/Dimensional - 24 to 30 years, average 27
Built-up - 17 to 25 years, average 20
Built-up and Gravel - 20 to 30 years, average 25
Concrete/Clay Tile - 40 to 60 years, average 50
Corrugated Asphalt - 9 to 13 years, average 11
EPDM (Rubber) - 20 to 30 years, average 23
Metal (Galvalume) - 30 to 50 years, average 40
Modified Bitumen - 10 to 17 years, average 15
Patio Cover - 20 to 30 years, average 25
PVC (Polyvinyl Chloride) - 20 to 30 years, average 25
Roll Roofing - 6 to 10 years, average 8
SPF (Spray Polyurethane Foam) - 20 to 50 years, average 30
TPO (Thermoplastic PolyOlefin) - 20 to 30 years, average 23

life expectancy

ROOF FLASHINGS, PENETRATIONS and COATINGS

Elastomeric Coating - 5 to 20 years, average 10
Flashing, Edge, Valley and Wall - 20 to 35 years, average 25
Flashing, Pipe Boots - 15 to 30, average 20
Gutter, Aluminum - 20 to 30 years, average 25
Gutter, Copper - 50+ years
Gutter, Vinyl - 10 to 25, average 15
Skylight and Light Tube - 8 to 20 years, average 14

SHUTTERS

Aluminum, exterior - 20 to 35 years, average 25
Aluminum, hurricane - 20 to 50 years, average 30
Vinyl plastic, exterior - 10 to 20 years, average 15
Vinyl plastic, interior - 10 to 25 years, average 20
Wood or composite, exterior - 10 to 20 years, average 15
Wood or composite, interior - 10 to 25 years, average 20

SIDING

Aluminum - 25 to 45 years, average 35
Brick - 100+ years
Engineered Wood Siding - 50+ years
Fiber-Cement Siding - 60+ years
Manufactured Stone - 50+ years
Plywood (T-111, RB&B, etc) - 20 to 50 years, average 35
Stucco on Block - 60 to 80+ years, average 70
Stucco or EIFS on Wood Frame - 50 to 70 years if maintained as necessary, average 60
Vinyl - 25 to 50 years, average 40
Wood or Composite - 20 to 40 years, average 30

life expectancy

SIDING

Aluminum - 25 to 45 years, average 35
Brick - 100+ years
Engineered Wood Siding - 50+ years
Fiber-Cement Siding - 60+ years
Manufactured Stone - 50+ years
Plywood (T-111, RB&B, etc) - 20 to 50 years, average 35
Stucco on Block - 60 to 80+ years, average 70
Stucco or EIFS on Wood Frame - 50 to 70 years, average 60
Vinyl - 25 to 50 years, average 40
Wood or Composite - 20 to 40 years, average 30

SITE

Driveway, Asphalt - 12 to 20 years, average 17
Driveway, Concrete - 25 to 45 years, average 35
Driveway, Concrete Resurfaced - 8 to 15 years, average 12
Driveway, Gravel - 4 to 10 years, average 5
Driveway, Paver - 25 to 45 years, average 35
Fence, Chain Link - 25 to 35 years, average 30
Fence, Vinyl - 20 to 35 years, average 25
Fence, Wood - 15 to 25 years, average 20
Mulch - 1 to 4 years, average 2
Retaining Wall, Timber Railroad Ties - 20 to 30 years, average 25
Retaining Wall, Dry-Stacked Stone - 50 to 100+ years, average 70
Sprinkler System - 20+ years
Termite Ground Treatment - 10+ years
Sprinkler Control Panel - 6 to 10 years, average 8
Sprinkler Underground Piping - 35 to 50 years, average 40
Sprinkler Valves - 10 to 15 years, average 12
Sprinkler Heads - 10 to 15 years, average 12
Walkway, Concrete - 25 to 50 years
Walkway, Gravel - 5 to 12 years, average 7

life expectancy

STAIRS

Interior Stairs - 100+ years
Interior Manufactured/Spiral Stairs - 100+ years
Exterior Concrete/Steel Steps/Stairs - 50 to 80 years, average 65
Exterior Wood Steps/Stairs - 15 to 35 years, average 25
Pull-Down Attic Ladder - 30 to 60 years, average 40

SWIMMING POOLS

Concrete - 25 to 40 years, average 30
Concrete Pool Interior Finish - 9 to 16 years, average 12
Fiberglass - 25 to 35 years, average 30
Fiberglass Pool Interior Finish - 14 to 18 years, average 15
Vinyl Liner - 7 to 10 years, average 8 years
Pool Pump and Filter - 8 to 11 years, average 10
Pool Heater - 8 to 11 years, average 10

TECHNOLOGY

Carbon monoxide (CO) Detector - 5 to 10 years
Combo Smoke/CO Detector - 7 to 10 years
Doorbell - 40 years
Radon Fan - 5 to 20 years, average 7
Radon Manometer (U-tube) - 10 years
Radon Piping - 50 to 70 years, average 60
Security System - 15 years
Smoke Detector - 10 years
WIFI network - 5 years

WALL STRUCTURAL SYSTEMS

Brick - 100+ years
Concrete (monolithic) - 100+ years
Concrete Block - 100+ years
ICF (Insulated Concrete Form) - 100+ years
Natural Stone - 100+ years
Wood Stud Frame - 100+ years

WELL and SEPTIC SYSTEMS

Septic Tank System - 25 to 40 years, average 30
Sewage Grinder Pump - 6 to 16 years, average 9
Water Softener - 9 to 16 years, average 12
Well - 20 to 50 years, average 35
Well Casing - 20 to 35 years, average 25
Well Pressure Tank - 10 to 25 years, average 15
Well Pump - 10 to 15 years, average 12

WINDOWS

Aluminum - 15 to 30 years, average 20
Double-Pane (Insulated) Glass - 10 to 20 years, average 15
Fiberglass - 20 to 45 years, average 35
Skylight and Light Tube - 8 to 20 years, average 14
Vinyl - 20 to 40 years, average 30
Window Blinds - 3 to 6 years
Wood - 20 to 45 years, average 30

life expectancy

site built codes

Building codes are useful to a home inspector as accepted and sensible safety standards. But they are also a slippery slope because codes are continuously evolving and changing with each new code edition. An older home cannot be expected to meet the standards for new construction, and this is especially true for electrical components.

So, where the information is available, we have noted in parentheses the year that newer code standards were issued. However, because national codes are not immediately adopted by local building jurisdictions, those dates may not be accurate for your location. It is not unusual for a building department to still be using a previous code edition, sometimes three or four editions back. HUD is an extreme example, still using the 2005 edition of NEC for manufactured homes built in 2023.

Other areas of the code, like stair and railing safety standards, are much more stable and longstanding. So codes are useful, but be careful if you quote them.

The codes cited are for what is likely to be observed during a visual inspection of an existing home. It is not intended to be an exhaustive listing and does not include areas that normally would only be visible for a home under construction. Also, some code standards are repeated if they are applicable for multiple categories.

Attics

❑ **Switched light** - required if attic is used for storage or if contains equipment that needs service. Light must be near equipment and switch near access opening (NEC).

❑ **Access opening required** - if attic areas exceeds 30 sq. ft. AND min. 30 in. measured from the top of the ceiling framing members to the bottom of the roof framing members (IRC)

❑ **Passageway to attic appliances** - max. 20 ft. from access to appliance, with solid floor min. 24 in. wide and 30 in high. (IRC).

❑ **Appliance service platform** - min. 30 in. square. Not required if can be serviced from opening (IRC).

❑ **Attic opening size** - min. 22 inches by 30 inches rough framed opening and min. 30 inches unobstructed headroom

site built codes

above opening. Must be large enough for removal of any installed equipment (IRC).

❏ **No truss web removal** - without repair, and repair specs approved by licensed engineer or manufacturer (IRC).

❏ **Inspector not required to enter attic** - or any unfinished spaces that are not readily accessible, or where entry could cause damage or, in the inspector's opinion, pose a safety hazard. (InterNACHI and ASHI)

Bathrooms

❏ **Ceiling height** - min. 6'-8". If sloped ceiling, then min. 7 ft. and no part less than 5 ft. Must be 6'-8" min. in shower, tub, and in front of toilet and sink (IRC).

❏ **Toilet min. clearances** - min. 15 in. from centerline of toilet to adjacent side wall or plumbing fixture at each side, with a total of 30-in. side-to-side. Min. 20 in. in front of toilet. Min. 6'-8" of height to ceiling at the center of required area in front of toilet where there is a sloped ceiling over toilet (IRC).

❏ **Hot water faucet handle must be on left** - as you face fixture/spigot for use (IRC).

❏ **Ventilation** - exhaust fan that terminates at exterior (not attic, 2006 IRC), or window with min. 1.5 sq. ft. clear opening (IRC).

Bathroom Shower

❏ **Single-handle anti-scald valve** required at shower. (2000 IRC)

❏ **Min. 30 in. interior dimensions** (IRC)

❏ **Finished floor to slope 1/4" to 1/2"** per foot to drain (IRC).

❏ **Shower walls non-absorbent** min. 72 in. above drain (IRC).

❏ **Shower door min. 22 in.** clear opening (IRC).

Electrical

Overhead Service Clearances

❏ **Over residential property and driveways on the property** - min. 12 ft. (NEC).

❏ **Over walking surfaces that are only accessible to pedestrians** - min. 10 ft. (NEC)

❑ **Over a roadway** - min. 18 ft. (NEC)

❑ **Over a roof low-slope roof, with less than 4/12 pitch** - min. 8 ft. (NEC)

❑ **Over a roof with 4/12 pitch or more** - min. 3 ft. (NEC)

❑ **Over a roof with 4/12 pitch or more, within 4 ft. of roof edge** - min. 18 in. (NEC)

❑ **Over decks and balconies** - min. 10 ft., including out 3 ft. (NEC).

❑ **At the sides and below an openable window** - 3 ft. min. (NEC)

❑ **Over a pool or outdoor spa** - min. 22.5 feet in any direction over water and within 10 ft. of edge of pool (NEC)

❑ **Only overhead service conductors** - can be attached to service mast (NEC)

Electrical Panels

❑ **Removal of dead front and examination of interior** - required by ASHI and several states, not required by InterNACHI.

❑ **Clothes closets** - panels not allowed (1981 NEC).

❑ **Bathrooms** - panels not allowed (1993 NEC).

❑ **Max. 6 switch-throws** to shut off service (1933 NEC)

❑ **Min. clearance in front of panel** - 36 in. deep by 30 in. wide (1978 NEC)

❑ **Neutrals not bonded** with grounds after service panel (1923 NEC)

❑ **Flush mount (recessed) panel** - no gap allowed between deadfront and surrounding surface of combustible (wood) wall, max. 1/4 in. for non-combustible (steel or concrete). Max. 1/8 in. gap around sides of box (NEC).

❑ **Max. breakers in panel** - Was 42 until 2008 NEC, now as specified by manufacturer (NEC).

❑ **No low-voltage wiring** - such as doorbell transformers, allowed in panel (NEC).

❑ **Breaker in "UP" position must be "ON"** - at breakers vertically mounted in panel (1975 NEC).

❑ **Highest breaker switch** - not more than 6'-7" above floor (NEC).

Receptacles
❑ **120-volt** - requires equipment ground, 3-slot (1962 NEC).
❑ **240-volt** - requires equipment ground, 4-slot (1999 NEC).
❑ **Balcony, deck, or porch** - min. one receptacle if within 4 in. of house (2020 NEC). Formerly only required if also directly accessible from inside home (NEC)
❑ **Closets** - not required.
❑ **Exterior** - min. one receptacle at front and back of house exterior, not more than 6.5 ft. above grade (2005 NEC). Formerly min. one receptacle (1971 NEC)
❑ **Bathrooms** - requires separate circuit, and min. one receptacle within 3 ft. of each sink (1996 NEC).
❑ **Foyers** - that are not part of a hallway and are greater than 60 sq. ft., min. one receptacle outlet on each wall space that is 3 ft. or more in width (NEC).
❑ **Garage** - min. one receptacle (NEC). Updated by 2020 NEC to one per vehicle bay (garage door).
❑ **Hallways** - min. one receptacle in a hallway that is 10 ft. or longer.
❑ **Kitchen counters** - requires 2 separate circuits (1959 NEC).
❑ **Laundry** - requires separate circuit, and min. one receptacle for laundry equipment (1971 NEC).
❑ **Living areas** - max. 12 ft. apart, max. 6 ft. from any point along base of wall 2 ft. or more long (1956 NEC).

AFCI - Arc Fault Circuit Interrupters
First required - for all bedroom receptacle outlets (NEC 2002).
Upgraded - to include family rooms, dining rooms, living rooms, parlors, libraries, dens, sunrooms, recreation rooms, closets, hallways, or similar rooms or areas (NEC 2008). Then kitchens and laundrys added (NEC 2014)
CAFCI - combination AFCIs replaces AFCIs (NEC 2008).

GFCI (Ground Fault Circuit Interrupter) location requirements
❑ **Bathrooms** - min. one receptacle within three feet of each sink on an adjacent wall, or inside or on the face of the sink cabinet not more than 12 inches below countertop (1975 NEC)

❏ **Crawl Spaces** - (1990 NEC)

❏ **Dishwashers** - (2014 NEC)

❏ **Disposals** - (2020 NEC)

❏ **Exterior** - (1975 NEC)

❏ **Garage** - (1975 NEC for receptacles below 6'-8" and excluding receptacles for dedicated appliances, then all receptacles in 2008 NEC)

❏ **Kitchen** - (1987 NEC within 6 ft. of sink, expanded to all kitchen counter receptacles in 1996 NEC).

❏ **Laundry and utility sinks** - receptacles within 6 ft. (2005 NEC)

❏ **Pool** - all receptacles within 20 ft. of pool edge (1996 NEC) and no receptacles within 6 ft of pool edge (2008 NEC)

❏ **Refrigerator** - if within 6 feet of a sink (2014 NEC)

❏ **Spa tub indoor** - required for receptacles within 10 ft. of tub, and no receptacles within 5 ft. (1987 NEC), and changed to no receptacles within 6 ft (2008 NEC)

❏ **Unfinished basements** - all receptacles (1990 NEC)

❏ **Wet bars** - all receptacles within 6 ft. of wet bar sink on counter (1993 NEC); then wet bar sinks, with or without counter (2005 NEC).

Switched Lighting

❏ **All habitable rooms** - must have switched lighting. Switched receptacle can substitute for installed light, except kitchens and bathrooms (NEC).

❏ **Clothes closets** - not required but, if installed, bare-bulb or partially enclosed incandescent bulbs and pendants not allowed. Enclosed incandescent and LED allowed min. 12 inches from any possible closet storage. Enclosed fluorescent min. 6 in. from closet storage space (NEC).

❏ **Exterior entrances** - min. one switched light at the exterior side of outdoor entrances doors to a dwelling unit, attached garage, and detached garage that has electric power. A vehicle door is not considered an outdoor entrance (NEC)

❏ **Hallways, stairways, attached garages** (also detached garages that have electrical power) - At least one switched light (NEC).

□ **Kitchens and bathrooms** - Must have switched installed lighting. Switched receptacle not allowed alternative (NEC).
□ **Occupancy sensor** - allowed if manual override (NEC).
□ **Stairways** - with six or more risers, required three-way switched lighting (NEC).

Egress Requirements
□ **Egress (exterior escape) doors** - min. one required. Must provide direct access from all living areas of the home to the exterior without traveling through a locked door or garage, and side-hinged with min. clear opening of 32 inches wide by 78 inches high. Other exterior doors can be smaller.
□ **No double-cylinder deadbolt locks -** at egress doors (UBC 1927, IRC)
□ **All exterior doors must have a landing** - not less than the width of the door by 36 inches in direction of travel, except when steps with two or fewer risers are located on either side of the door. (IRC)
□ **Security bars -** allowed over emergency egress doors and windows if such devices are releasable or removable from the inside without the use of a key, tool, special knowledge or force greater than that required for the normal operation (IRC).
□ **Egress windows** - one required at each sleeping room. Min. clear opening 20 inches wide by 24 inches high, and min. 5.7 sq. ft. Max. window sill ht. 44 inches (IRC).

Gutters
□ **Roofs with less than 6" overhang** - gutters with downspouts required (IRC).
□ **Areas with expansive or collapsible soil** - gutters or other water disposal system required that deposits water min. 5 ft. from foundation.

HVAC
□ **Exhaust duct must terminate at exterior** - for dryer, bathroom, and kitchen range hood fans (IRC).
□ **Installed heat** - required for all habitable rooms. Portable

site built codes

space heaters not acceptable (IRC).

❑ **No duct openings allowed in garage** - unless system serves only garage (IRC).

❑ **Single wall vent for gas furnace** - min. 6 inches from flammable materials (IRC).

❑ **Gas appliance connector** - max. 1 and max. 6 ft. long, only in accessible location and entire length visible, not where subject to damage, cannot connect directly to LP-gas tank (AMI).

❑ **Clearance at service side** - of furnace, air handler, or condenser min. 30 inches wide by 36 inches deep.

❑ **Service receptacle required** - 125-volt and GFCI, within 25 feet of HVAC equipment (NEC)

❑ **No fuel-burning furnaces allowed** - at bedrooms, bathrooms, or closet opening onto bedroom or bathroom, or closet with storage. Exception for sealed compartment (IRC).

❑ **Disconnect within sight** - for condenser, furnace, or air handler. Can be at panel if within sight (1978 NEC).

❑ **Wall or window air conditioners require dedicated circuit** - if marked "USE ON SINGLE OUTLET CIRCUIT ONLY" on data sticker (NEC).

❑ **Wall or window air conditioners not required to be inspected** - unless permanently attached and require tools for removal (ASHI and InterNACHI standards).

Plumbing

Fixture Tailpieces, Traps, and Trap Arms

❑ **Trap seal** - min. 2 in., max. 4 in. (IRC).

❑ **Traps types not allowed** - "S" trap, bell trap, crown traps, drum traps, any trap with interior partition or moving parts IRC).

❑ **Corrugated or flexible traps, tailpieces, or trap arms** - not allowed. Must be smooth and self-cleaning. (IRC).

❑ **Trap arm size** - same as trap (IRC).

❑ **Trap arm length** - min. 2 times pipe diameter (IRC).

❑ **Trap arm slope** - min. slope 1/4" per foot, or 1/8" for 3" dia. or larger (IRC).

❑ **Double trap** - not allowed (IRC).

❑ **Building traps** - not allowed (IRC).

❑ **Venting** - all traps require vent. Vent opening must be at or above trap seal (IRC).

❑ **Vent termination** - min. 6 in. above roof, or 2 inches above solar panels (IRC).

❑ **Air admittance valve** - min. 4 in. above fixture drain (IRC).

❑ **Vent to outdoors** - min. one when using air admittance valves (IRC).

❑ **Air admittance valve in attic** - min. 6 in. above insulation (IRC).

❑ **Sinks and lavatories** - strainer required (IRC).

❑ **Hot and cold water required** - at sinks, lavs, showers, tubs, and bidets (IRC).

Water supply piping

❑ **PVC** - not allowed for distribution pipe inside home (IRC).

❑ **CPVC at water heater** - min. 6 in. from draft hood and flue connector of tank-type water heater (IRC).

❑ **PEX** - not installed where exposed to direct or indirect sunlight (AMI).

❑ **PEX at water heater** - No PEX pipe within first 18 in. of tank-type water heater (IRC).

❑ **Insulation required for hot water supply pipe in unconditioned locations** - such as attic, crawl space, or exterior (IRC).

❑ **Insulation required for supply pipe in unconditioned locations** - where winter design temperature is 32° or lower (IRC).

❑ **Saddle valves** - puncture type valves not allowed (IRC).

Roofing

Minimum Slope

❑ **Asphalt shingles** - min. 2:12 pitch, but below 4:12 requires double underlayment, which is not readily determinable (IRC).

❑ **Clay and concrete tile** - min. 2.5:12 pitch, but below 4:12 requires double underlayment, which is not readily determinable (IRC)

❑ **Metal Shingles** - min. 3:12 pitch (IRC).

❑ **Mineral Surface Roll Roofing** - min. 1:12 pitch (IRC).

❑ **Slate** - min. 4:12 pitch (IRC).

❑ **Wood shingles** - min. 3:12 pitch (IRC).
❑ **Wood shakes** - min. 3:12 pitch (IRC).
❑ **Built-up** - min. 1/4:12 pitch (IRC).
❑ **Metal lapped panels** - without lap sealant, min. 3:12 pitch; with lap sealant, 1/2:12 pitch (IRC).
❑ **Metal standing seam** - min. 1/4:12 pitch (IRC).
❑ **Modified bitumen** - min. 1/4:12 pitch (IRC).
❑ **Thermoset single ply (EPDM)** - min. 1/4:12 pitch (IRC).
❑ **Thermoplastic single ply (TPO, PVC)** - min. 1/4:12 pitch (IRC).
❑ **Sprayed Polyurethane Foam (SPF)** - min. 1/4:12 pitch (IRC).

Room Size

❑ **Habitable room size** - min. 70 sq. ft. and min. 7 ft. wide at smallest dimension. Habitable rooms must have a heat source (IRC).
❑ **Not classed as habitable rooms** - kitchens, bathrooms, laundry rooms, bath/toilet rooms, closets, halls, storage or utility areas (IRC).

Site

❑ **Ground slope around home** - min. 6 inches in first 10 feet (IRC).
❑ **Hardscape slope** - min. 2% within 10 feet (IRC).
❑ **Trees, site grading, drainage, and retaining walls** - only required to examine and report where may adversely affect the building (InterNACHI, ASHI).

Smoke/CO Alarms

❑ **Smoke detector/alarms** - required in each sleeping room, outside each sleeping room (hallway or other room), and one in each additional story, hardwired with battery backup (1991 UBC, all IRC). Formerly in hallway only, with battery acceptable (1971 UBC).
❑ **CO detector/alarms** - located within 10 ft. of each sleeping room of home with fireplace, fuel burning appliance, or garage.

Combo alarms okay (IRC). Required in new homes and remodels in most states, and in Florida since 2008.

Stairs

❑ **Width** - min. 36 in. measured above handrail (IRC).
❑ **Risers** - max. riser 7-3/4 in. (IRC)
❑ **Open risers** - must prevent passage of 4 in. sphere, except if less than 30 in. above floor or spiral stair (IRC).
❑ **Tread** - min. 10 in., or 11 in. if no nosing (IRC)
❑ **Max. deviation** - between treads or risers is 3/8 in. (IRC)
❑ **Nosing projection** - min. 3/4 in., max. 1-1/4" in. (IRC)
❑ **Headroom** - min. 6'-8" (IRC).

Winding Stairs

Winder tread - min. 10 in. at walkline, which is 12 in. from inside of curve (IRC).
Rectangular tread - not required to match winders (IRC).

Spiral Stairs

Risers - max. 9-1/2 in. (IRC)
Tread - min. 6-3/4 in. at walkline (IRC)
Width - min. 26 in. at and below handrail (IRC)
Headroom - min. 6'-6" at walkline (IRC)

Stair Lighting

Required - for stairs and landings (IRC).
Exterior stairs - lighting required at top and bottom landings. Interior stairs - require light switch at each floor level if 6 or more risers. Automatic sensor or remote acceptable alternative (IRC).

Stair Handrails

❑ **Required** - on min. one side of stairs with 4 or more risers, 34 to 38 in. above nosing.
❑ **Space to wall** - max. 4-1/2 in., min. 1-1/2 in. Must be graspable and ends must return to wall or adjacent surface, or volute okay.

Guardrails

❏ **Required** - min. 36 in. high at walking surface with open side more than 30 in. above adjacent lower surface within 36 in. horizontally.
❏ **Openings** - must obstruct 4 in. sphere at open sides, and 6 in. sphere at triangle below bottom rail.

Termite Protection
❏ **Exterior clearance to non-PT wood** - min. 6 in. ground clearance around base of exterior walls, min. 2 in. at hardscape (IRC).
❏ **Crawl space clearance to non-PT wood** - min. 12 in. to beam bottoms, and 18 in. to joist bottoms (IRC).

Water Heaters
❏ **TPR valve** - temperature and pressure relief valve required (1976 UPC, all IRC).
❏ **TPR discharge piping** - must for rated for use (not PVC), not smaller than outlet of valve, must drain by gravity and not trapped, no valves or T fittings (IRC).
❏ **TPR piping termination** - termination must be readily visible, not cause injury, not threaded or capped, not more than 6 in. or less than 2 pipe diameters above surface below (IRC).
❏ **No fuel-burning water heaters allowed** - at bedrooms, bathrooms, or closet opening onto bedroom or bathroom, or closet with storage. Exception for sealed compartment (IRC).
❏ **Fuel water heater at garage** - min. 18 in. above floor unless rated for floor installation (IRC).
❏ **Single wall vent for gas water heater** - min. 6 in. from flammable materials (IRC).
❏ **FVIR (flammable vapor ignition resistant)** - required for fuel water heaters (CPSC 2003).
❏ **Thermal expansion tank** - required for tank water heaters (2006 IRC)
❏ **Electric water heater disconnect** - must be within sight or lockout device at breaker in panel (NEC).

❑ **Electric water heater working space** - min. 30 in. wide by 36 in. deep at service side (NEC).

❑ **Clearance at service side** - min. 30 in. wide by 36 in. deep for electric (NEC), 24 in. square for gas (IRC).

❑ **Water heater shut-off valve** - must be full-open type (IRC).

❑ **PEX pipe** - No PEX pipe within first 18 in. of tank-type water heater (IRC).

❑ **Thermal expansion tank at water heater** - required for closed water distribution systems (2006 IRC)

❑ **Gas appliance connector** - max. 1 and max. 6 ft. long, only in accessible location and entire length visible, not where subject to damage, cannot connect directly to LP-gas tank (AMI).

site built codes

manufactured codes

Any time you want to refer directly to the codes, they are available free online.

❑ **HUD-Code for home construction:**
https://www.ecfr.gov/current/title-24/subtitle-B/chapter-XX/part-3280
❑ **HUD-Code for home installation:**
https://www.ecfr.gov/current/title-24/subtitle-B/chapter-XX/part-3285
❑ **Florida code for installation/construction, including "Florida Overrides":**
https://www.flrules.org/gateway/organization.asp?id=42
and then select 15C-1 and 15C-2

Anchors and Tie-Downs

❑ **Anchor heads and stabilizer plates** - bottom of head and top of stabilizer plate should be flush with the ground.
❑ **Anchor straps** - must be free of corrosion.
❑ **Tie-down spacing** - varies according to wind zone and age of home. Older homes spaced 8 to 10 ft. apart. Newer standard in Florida less than 6 feet.

Belly Board

❑ **Must be continuous** - and seal the underside of home from moisture. Any tears or holes, typically due to plumbing repairs or animals under home, require repair. Also called belly wrap or bottom board.

Crawl Space

❑ **Ground Cover Vapor Barrier** - required when crawl space enclosed by skirting for new homes since 2008. Exception when in area with dry soil conditions. Must be 6 mil polyethylene or equivalent, with 12 in. overlap at seams. Not required under porches, decks, or recessed entries.

Data Plate

❏ **Must be permanently affixed** - near electrical panel or other readily visible location. Possible locations are master bedroom closet wall or inside of kitchen cabinet door under sink. See page 58 for details.

Electrical

❏ **Service panel** - must be min. 100 amps, within 30 ft. of home and within sight.
❏ **No aluminum branch circuit conductors** - including multistrand aluminum for appliance circuits.
❏ **AFCI not required** - but, if installed, must meet 2005 NEC.

Emergency Egress

All homes leave the factory meeting these emergency exit safety standards, but they are sometimes voided by homeowner remodeling and additions.
❏ **Doors** - min. 2 exterior doors for emergency egress, max. 12 ft. apart single-wide, and 20 ft. apart double-wide. One of doors must be max. 35 ft. from door of each bedroom. Travel cannot require passage thru lockable interior door.

Door must have a minimum 28 in. by 72 in. clear opening. Sliding glass door acceptable.

All homes leave the factory meeting these emergency exit safety standards, but they are often by homeowner remodeling and additions.
❏ **Stairs** - required at each exit door, min. full width of door opening, and compliant with local code.
❏ **Bedroom Windows** - must be at min. 22 inches in the horizontal or vertical least dimension and at least five square feet in area, the bottom of the window opening be not more than 36 inches above the floor, and the locks and latches which need to be operated to permit exiting not be located more than 54 inches above the finished floor. The five square feet must be a clear open area, and it must open directly to the exterior. Also, there is an exemption if the sleeping room has a HUD-code exterior door.

Exhaust Fans

☐ **Bathroom** - min. 50 cfm, terminate at exterior.

☐ **Kitchen** - min. 100 cfm, terminate at exterior.

☐ **Whole house** - must be between 50 and 90 cfm. Usually either a low volume exhaust fan in ceiling of hallway or fresh-air intake duct at air handler.

Florida Overrides of HUD-Code

Here's some examples of

☐ **Wood foundations** - are not allowed.

☐ **Tie-down straps must be double-dip** - (0.60 oz. per sq. ft.) galvanized. HUD allows 0.30 oz. per sq. ft.

☐ **Tie-down max. spacing of 5'-4"** - if manufacturer's instructions not available, and must be attached to top of beam.

☐ **Piers are required near each end of the home's centerline** - whether or not the manufacturer requires them.

☐ **Minimum height from ground to bottom of frame I-beam is 18-inches** - except that 25% of area can be lower, but not below 12-inches clearance. HUD allows lower.

☐ **Piers over 52-inches high must be engineered** - HUD accepts up to 80-inches before engineering necessary.

Home Additions, Site Built

☐ **Cannot bear on manufactured home** - Unless manufacturer has installed host beam in wall and foundation upgraded. Will be noted on data plate.

☐ **Must comply with local building codes** - and requires permit.

☐ **Addition cannot obstruct egress windows or doors** - that open directly to exterior.

HUD Tag (also called Certification Label or Red Tag)

☐ **Must be permanently affixed** - to the taillight end of each transportable section. Metal plate stamped with 3 letters indicating state, then 6 digit sequential unique serial number.

HVAC
❑ **Flexible ducts in crawlspace** - must be supported above the ground by straps or other means max. 4 feet apart.

IBTS
❑ The Institute for Building Technology and Safety (IBTS) maintains a data base with all the construction information on manufactured homes built since HUD took over supervision on July 15, 1976. So they are the people to contact if a homebuyer needs to find out or verify any information about a used home, such as:

•• The VIN/serial number, if you give them a HUD tag (Verification Label) number.

•• The HUD tag number(s), if you give them the serial number. But IBTS does not issue replacement HUD tag.

•• A replacement for a missing HUD Performance Certification sheet (data plate), if you provide either the serial number or the HUD tag number(s).

You can order any of the items from their website at www.ibts.org and, of course, there is a fee—and an additional fee if you want rush service.

Piers - Common Defects
❑ **Concrete blocks sit on pad in wrong direction** - for pads that are not square, the long side of block must be parallel to long side of pad.
❑ **Pier blocks are not perpendicular to I-beam or centerline** - load not distributed correctly if blocks are parallel to I-beam or centerline.
❑ **Voids in block not facing upward** - Concrete block has significantly less load-bearing strength when voids are facing sideways.
❑ **Block pier not centered on pad** - Must be centered to distribute load correctly.

mfr. home code

❑ **Block pier not centered under I-beam** - Again, important for load distribution.

❑ **Block piers too tall** - Single block piers cannot exceed 36-inches, measured from top of pad or footing to top of concrete block stack, including 4-inch cap block. Reduced to 24-inches at corners. All piers over 36-inches and corner piers over 24-inches must be double-stacked block. Piers over 52-inches must have engineering specs.

❑ **Block piers too short** - Minimum distance allowed between ground and bottom of I-beam is 18-inches except that, when the grade is sloped, 25% of the area can be lower—but not below 12-inches. This is a "Florida over-ride" that exceeds 12-inch minimum crawl space clearance under a home allowed by HUD.

❑ **Block piers leaning** - Horizontal offset from top of bottom of pier cannot exceed 1-inch.

❑ **Blocks cracked or chipped** - Fractures or otherwise damaged block not acceptable.

❑ **Cap blocks wrong size or wrong material** - Can only be approved material, such as solid (no voids) 4-inch concrete block, pressure-treated wood 2x8, or approved plastic caps.

❑ **Shims incorrectly installed** - Shim stack can be no more than 1-inch high under new home, or 1-1/2 inches under used home. Stack must align.

❑ **Missing perimeter piers** - required on both sides of side wall exterior doors (such as entry, patio, and sliding glass doors) and any other side wall openings of 48 inches or greater in width, and under load-bearing porch posts, factory installed fireplaces, and fireplace stoves)

Room Size

❑ **Bedrooms** - No dimension less than 5 ft., min. 50 sq. ft., bedrooms for 2 or more 70 sq. ft.

❑ **Bedroom closet** - min. 22 in. deep with rod and shelf.

❑ **Living room** - min. 150 sq. ft.

❑ **Overall size** - min. 400 sq. ft.

❏ **Ceiling height** - min. 7'-0" for 50% of floor area and min. 5'-0" for remainder. Min. under dropped beams and ducts 6'-4". Hallways and foyers min. 6'-4".
❏ **Hallways** - min. width 28 in.

Site

❏ **Grade** - All drainage must be diverted away from the home, and grade must slope 1/2" per foot for first 10 feet. If not possible, then drains or swales must be added. Typically, a pad is necessary. No low areas where water can accumulate under home.

Smoke Alarms

❏ **Must be installed** - on any wall in the hallway or living area outside each sleeping room, and also in each sleeping room. Homes with bedroom areas that are separated require a smoke alarm for each area. They must be interconnected.

The smoke alarms may be wired to house power with a battery backup, or alarms with a 10-year battery only are an acceptable alternative. Also, combination smoke and CO (carbon monoxide) alarms are allowed.

Formerly, a smoke alarm was only required in each hall or area outside each bedroom, hard-wired without a battery backup required.

Vehicle Identification Number (VIN)

❏ **Location** - Stamped in the front steel beam cross-member under the home (the beam that the tow hitch is bolted onto, perpendicular to the long side of the mobile home). Also on paper data plate inside home.

Data Plate (also called Performance Certificate)

The HUD Performance Certificate is a paper sticker attached to an interior surface of the home. It's often referred to as the "data plate" and provides the home's construction specifications. It has been required by HUD since they took over the supervision of manufactured home construction in June, 1976.

The data plate is usually found in one of these four locations: 1) wall of the master bedroom closet, 2) back of one of the kitchen cabinet doors, 3) side wall of the base cabinet under the kitchen sink, or 4) back of a hinged wood door covering the electric panel.

Here's an outline of the data you can retrieve and where to find it:

1. The name of the manufacturer and the location of the factory where it was produced.

2. The date of manufacture.
The year of manufacture is important, because construction standards were strengthened over the years, especially after certain key dates. Between June, 1976, (beginning of HUD Code) and July, 1994, all mobile homes were required to meet a single minimum standard. HUD has raised the standards several times since then.

3. A listing of the certification label numbers (also called HUD tag numbers) affixed to each transportable section of the home.
One number for a single-wide, two for a double-wide, and so forth. They should match the numbers found on the metal tags riveted to the outside wall of the home.

4. The manufacturer's serial number and model designation of the home.
In some versions of the data plate, the model designation is in a separate box.

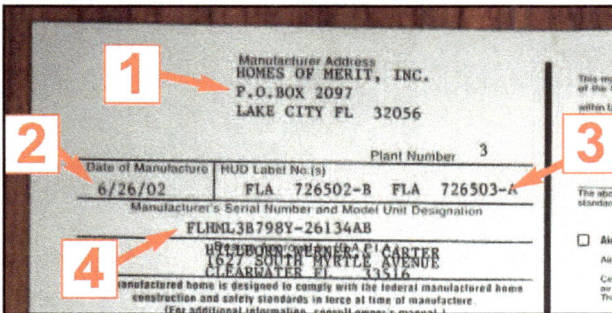

5. A list of the factory-installed equipment, including the manufacturer's name and model number.
Comparing this list with the refrigerator, range, water heater, and other currently installed appliances in the home will tell you whether they are original to the construction or newer.

6. A check-box for the "wind load zone" in which the home was designed to be located.

Zones are I, II, and III—with II and III zones constructed to withstand hurricane-force winds. Zone 3 is for the higher hurricane winds in South Florida and southeastern coastal areas. Here too, compare the wind load zone checked with the adjacent map to verify proper construction for the where the home is located. A home designed for a higher number wind zone can be located in a lower zone, but a number lower than the zone of the location is not acceptable. Also, there is no Zone I in Florida, so a Zone I home cannot be located to Florida

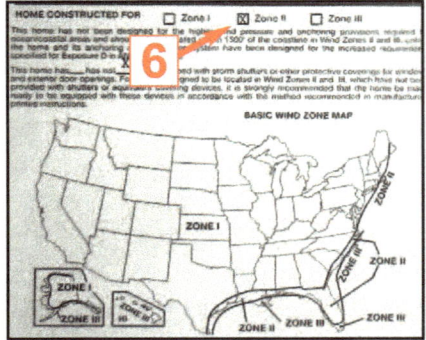

7. A check-box for the "roof load zone" in which the home was designed to be located.
Northern roof load zones are meant to allow for a snow load. Compare the roof load zone checked with the adjacent small U.S. map to confirm that the home meets the standard for where it is located.

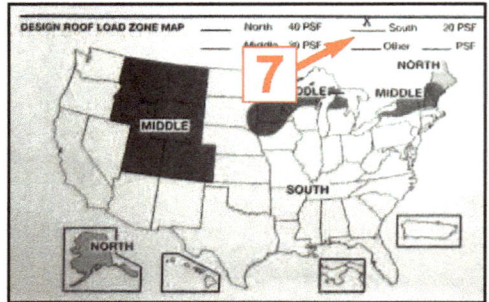

8. Heating and cooling data and "thermal map."
This shows the zone the home was designed to be located in, along with a calculation of the level of heat transmission of the building envelope. Sometimes this is a separate plate. A home designed for a higher number thermal zone can be located in a lower zone, but not vice-versa.

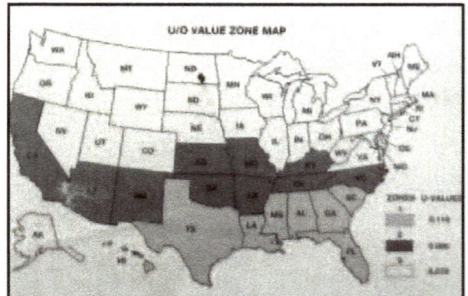

What heating or cooling equipment was factory-installed in the home is also noted, with BTU rating. If no cooling system was factory installed, a recommended size unit is stated in BTUs. It is stated as "up to," meaning the number is a recommended maximum. Some homeowners replace their old air conditioner with one far above the BTUs of the manufacturer's recommendation, which can cause moisture problems in the home. So it's worth noting in your report when you see a significantly oversized air conditioner.

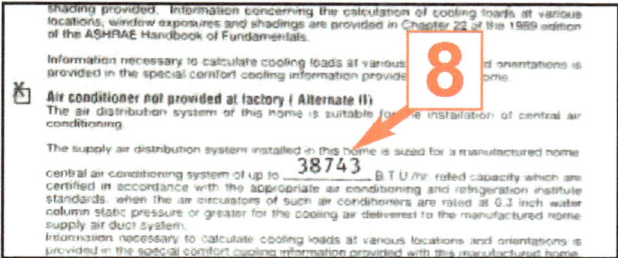

The rating of the home's insulation is in U-value, which many homebuyers are unfamiliar with. To present the insulation data, if requested, we recommend converting to the more familiar R-value, which is the multiplication inverse of U-values. So a U-value of .058 is $1 \div .058 = 17$.

Unfortunately, the data plate is often missing in older homes. If the homebuyer needs any of the data plate info for financing or insurance, it can be retrieved from IBTS (Institute for Business and Tecnology Safety) by filing a request at their website at www.ibts.org. You will need to give them the HUD tag number or serial number and pay a fee to receive it. See page 85 to learn more.

www.ingramcontent.com/pod-product-compliance
Lightning Source LLC
Chambersburg PA
CBHW051259020426
42333CB00026B/3284